Families We Keep

LGBTQ People and Their Enduring Bonds with Parents

Rin Reczek *and* Emma Bosley-Smith

NEW YORK UNIVERSITY PRESS
New York

NEW YORK UNIVERSITY PRESS
New York
www.nyupress.org

References to Internet websites (URLs) were accurate at the time of writing. Neither the author nor New York University Press is responsible for URLs that may have expired or changed since the manuscript was prepared.

Library of Congress Cataloging-in-Publication Data
Names: Reczek, Rin, author. | Bosley-Smith, Emma, author.
Title: Families we keep : LGBTQ people and their enduring bonds with parents / Rin Reczek and Emma Bosley-Smith.
Description: New York : New York University Press, [2022] | Includes bibliographical references and index.
Identifiers: LCCN 2021025433 | ISBN 9781479813322 (hardback ; alk. paper) | ISBN 9781479813339 (paperback ; alk. paper) | ISBN 9781479813346 (ebook) | ISBN 9781479813353 (ebook other)
Subjects: LCSH: Sexual minorities' families. | Sexual minorities—Family relationships. | Dysfunctional families. | Parent and child. | Parent and adult child.
Classification: LCC HQ73 .R43 2022 | DDC 306.85086/6—dc23
LC record available at https://lccn.loc.gov/2021025433

New York University Press books are printed on acid-free paper, and their binding materials are chosen for strength and durability. We strive to use environmentally responsible suppliers and materials to the greatest extent possible in publishing our books.

Manufactured in the United States of America

10 9 8 7 6 5 4 3 2 1

Also available as an ebook

CONTENTS

GLOSSARY

AGENDER: A person who does not have a gender; a person who eschews gender labels

ASEXUAL: A person who experiences little to no sexual attraction to other people; a person who identifies as asexual, demisexual, semisexual, and other asexual identities

BISEXUAL: A person who is attracted to men and women; a person who is attracted to people of any gender

CISGENDER: A person whose assigned sex and/or assigned gender at birth aligns with their sex and/or gender identity and expression today

CISHET: Shorthand for a person who is both cisgender and heterosexual

GENDER EXPANSIVE: An inclusive name for a group of people who are not cisgender; a person who eschews gender labels; a person who slides among different non-cisgender identities including trans, gender queer, gender non-conforming, and enby

GENDERQUEER (GQ): A person who eschews the binary sex and gender system; a person whose gender identity and expression lie outside of the gender categories of man and woman

GENDER NONBINARY (GNB, ENBY) GENDER NONCONFORMING (GNC): A person whose gender expression and identity differs from or lies outside of the gender categories of man and woman; a person who does not assign a gender to themselves; a person who eschews the gender binary and gender labels

HETEROSEXUAL/STRAIGHT: A person who is primarily attracted to and has intimate relationships with people of a different sex and/or gender; a person with a heterosexual or straight identity

LGBTQ: Lesbian, gay, bisexual, transgender, queer, and other gender and sexual minoritized identities; we use "LGBTQ" as shorthand to refer to gender and sexual minoritized people or those who do not identify as cisgender or heterosexual, even as not all identities are represented in the letters of this acronym

PANSEXUAL: A person who is attracted to, and/or has sexual relationships with, people of any gender; a person who identifies as pansexual

TRANSGENDER: A person whose sex and/or gender identity and expression are other than their sex and/or gender assigned at birth; someone who identifies with a trans identity including trans woman, trans man, or transgender[1]

Note: This is not an exhaustive list of gender and sexuality categories and identities. Instead, this list should be viewed as terms the interviewees in this study use to explain their own personal identities within their current historical, social, and political context. These terms are forever shifting in both historical time and geographic space, with new terms emerging and old terms changing meaning or falling out of favor.[2]

Introduction

The Parent Trap

When she was nine, Vicky realized she was attracted to girls. But, Vicky's budding sexuality was crowded out by her overwhelming experiences of racism as a Black teen living in a predominantly white Midwestern town. "The big thing was that I didn't have an identity," Vicky, now a forty-seven-year-old gay cisgender woman, explains. The kids in Vicky's school taunted her because of her dark skin and ostracized her for using African American Vernacular English. "The struggle was on so many different levels from skin color to just overall identity with who I was," Vicky laments. "All of that played into me acting out and always trying to just fit in." Vicky didn't have time, energy, or resources to think about the fact that she liked girls.

Alongside constant racism at school, her home life further stunted her sexual awakening. Following her parents' divorce when Vicky was four, Vicky went to live with her mom and grandparents. Vicky rarely saw her dad after he quickly remarried and had two children with another woman. In her new home environment, Vicky's mother and grandparents emphasized the importance of being seen as a "normal" and "respectable" religious Black family. "As in most homes of people of color in the South upper middle class," she explains, "you're expected to get married after you get out of college, have children, be a part of the church." Vicky conformed to her family's standards by doing "the typical": getting married to a man, having children, and ignoring her attraction to women.

It wasn't until she was in her thirties—after her father passed away, her kids became teens, and she went through her own divorce—that

Vicky started to come to terms with her sexuality. "I think emotionally a milestone was coming to the realization that I needed to address where I was and begin to entertain, 'Okay, I like looking at a woman . . .' Then acting upon it. Then marrying a woman." When she told her mom and grandma about her new identity and partner, the triad's relationship changed irrevocably. Their response was "like, 'WHAT!?' It broke them," and it especially shocked her mom. "It was very challenging for my mother because the first thing she said was, 'You are not a lesbian,'" Vicky recalls. After the initial disbelief and denial, her mom condemned Vicky's sexuality, telling Vicky she was going to hell, that her kids would be socially and spiritually bankrupt, and that she would ruin her family's respectable reputation they worked so hard to maintain.

This rejection and shaming continue today, making the relationship between Vicky and her mom, in Vicky's words, "not good whatsoever." They are still regularly in touch, but their relationship remains on a surface level. "That guilt, that shame, that emotional blackmail—that persisted," creating a deep barrier between the two. Vicky's mom remains profoundly homophobic and "still harbor[s] those feelings of me being gay." And yet, coming out engendered Vicky's own self-acceptance and love—something she had always longed for. "It was also relieving because now I'm like, oh, I can be who I am. I can be okay with who I'm attracted to. So, it was freeing yet confining or stressful because of that duality of the situation."

Still, despite the rejection from and strain with her mom, Vicky's intergenerational tie persists. When asked why this tie continues despite the homophobia and conflict, Vicky explains, like so many people we will introduce you to throughout this book, that she just can't stop talking to her mom. "I can't not care about my grandma or my mom or my sister. That's a full-blown, I'm not going to say obligation, that's part of it, but that's a compulsory caring to me. I have to."

Till Death Do Us Part

There is no "till death do us part" vow between parents and children. And yet, as Vicky shows us, parent-child relationships are far more enduring than the marital relationships that made this phrase famous. The lifelong parent-child tie is so taken for granted that it doesn't need an oath. This unspoken pledge is our birthright; in times of good and bad, sickness and health, parents and children are bound for life.

This bond begins when we come into this world completely dependent on our parents for survival. Parents are expected to give us the essentials to grow, such as food, clothing, and a place to call home. They are charged with teaching us about language, relationships, emotions, and beliefs.[1] As we get older, relationships with our parents evolve. We gain more freedom to make our own choices about where to live, who to love, and how to make a living. But the influence of parents never really ends. Even in adulthood, parents remain primary to our everyday experiences and personal identity.

But what happens when parent-child relationships are less than good or even damaging? Do *these* ties end once kids become adults? The research says no. If you had a "not good whatsoever" friend, would you continue to hang out with them? See them for holidays? Stress over what they think of you? If you dated someone you didn't like all that much, would you keep going out together? Or if you married someone who continuously belittled you or put you down, would you stay in the marriage? Decades of research show that most difficult social ties—from friends to romantic partners—don't last.[2] The parent-child bond uniquely persists.

What makes the parent–adult child relationship so special? To get an answer to our question of why (and how) parent-child relationships are maintained even if they are strained, we talked to seventy-six lesbian, gay, bisexual, transgender, queer, pansexual, and other gender and sexually expansive adults (hereafter, LGBTQ) and forty-four of their parents (see the glossary for a list of key terms and definitions).[3] Why do we focus on LGBTQ adults and their parents to answer our question? While some parents are genuinely supportive of their child's LGBTQ identity and are advocates for their LGBTQ children,[4] Vicky's story is an illustration of how many parents disapprove of and reject their LGBTQ kids.[5] Despite this, remarkably, the vast majority of relationships between LGBTQ adults and their parents remain intact. Even Kath Weston, famous for detailing the importance of "chosen families" made up of lovers and friends, notes that most LGBTQ people *also* maintain their relationships with their parents. [6] Because of this unique position, LGBTQ people have a version of an "outsider-within" perspective,[7] where "a social group's placement in a specific, historical context of . . . inequality might influence its point of view on the world."[8] As outsiders-within, LGBTQ people exist as *part of* the family due to their history and position as children, but they also can be an *outsider* in the family due to homo-, trans-, bi-, and queer-phobia. Those who have the most challenging relationships with parents—who are both insiders and outsiders in the family—offer a view into the ties that bind together all parents and adult kids. We tell the stories of outsiders-within like Vicky who explain with such clarity *why* and *how* they stay in their parent-adult child relationships.[9]

We discuss our methods and interviewee characteristics in the methodological appendix. There, you'll also find the interview guides and descriptions of both Rin's and Emma's personal stakes and positionality in this project. But we want to mention a few things for context here before you read this book. First, some notes on language. "Cishet" is often used to refer to cisgender heterosexual people.[10] We use "trans" as shorthand for "transgender"; "gender nonbinary," "gender nonconforming," and "genderqueer" are simplified to "GNB" or "enby," "GNC," and "GQ", respectively. When talking about the interviewees as a whole, we use the term "LGBTQ" as shorthand. We explain these identity groups further in the glossary, but it's important to note that language changes over time, and these terms and definitions are a product of the historical moment within which this book was written, as well as a reflection of our specific sample of people. Second, since the LGBTQ population is by no means a monolith, we sought to represent a wide variety of gender and sexuality identities in this book. Thirty-six percent of the sample identifies as what we call gender expansive.[11] This category includes identities such as trans, GQ, GNC, enby/GNB, and we pay special attention to these interviewees' stories throughout the book because of the unique insight they bring. We also pay particular attention to stories of Black people, Latinx people, Indigenous people, Asian people, and other people of color. People of color have been historically left out of much research on LGBTQ families and we aim to add to the literature correcting this oversight. Additionally, privileging the voices of people of color, who inhabit a unique social location in our white supremacist society, unearths imperative truths that expand our understanding of family in profound ways.

Third, after we interviewed each LGBTQ adult, we asked them to connect us to one or more parent for a separate interview. But, not all kids wanted their parents interviewed, especially people who had particularly damaged relationships with their parents. Therefore, we show the parents' perspectives when relevant, but the LGBTQ adults are the focus of this book. And, finally, before we dive into the lives of the people we talked with, all of whom have been given pseudonyms, we want to mention that some individuals in our sample had neglectful parents; experienced sexual, emotional, financial, and physical abuse; lived in poverty; experienced being unhoused; and discussed other sensitive events and topics. We include many of these details to help our readers understand our interviewees' experiences. But we also know that reading these accounts may remind our readers of dark spots in their own lives. Please take care as you read the rest of this book and reach out to a trusted person if the need arises.

Book Overview

Part I: Why LGBTQ Adults Stay in the Family: The Power of Compulsory Kinship

Part I of this book starts with theorizing *why* adults stay in bonds with parents by introducing our core concept, compulsory kinship, followed by empirical illustrations of compulsory kinship's rationales. First, in chapter 1 "Compulsory Kinship," we explain what compulsory kinship is, its origins, its consequences for everyday family life in the United States, and how it operates in relationships between LGBTQ adult children and their parents.

Compulsory kinship is a straightforward concept that calls attention to the fact that most people stay in parent-adult child relationships not by individual choice but because of intense social forces that constrain us so much we don't have much choice at all. The word "compulsory" means forced, obligatory, and coercive. Compulsory forces are those that structure our everyday lives and mask the broader influences that constrain our individual decisions.[12] For example, the decision to have children is not just an individual choice but a result of social, familial, and governmental pronatalist pressures and constraints that shape individual beliefs and behaviors around fertility.[13] You can never really know if your desire to have children is *yours*, or a product of your broader environment, because the two are forever entwined. The same is true with the decision to stay connected with your parents in adulthood. Such compulsory forces are what Vicky is talking about in the opening of this chapter, actually using the word "compulsory" to explain why she keeps her bond to her homophobic mom.

The term "kinship" refers to a culturally defined relationship between people who are thought of as family.[14] As Weston writes, in the United States, "biology is a defining feature of kinship . . . blood ties make certain people kin, regardless of whether those individuals display the love and enduring solidarity expected to characterize familial relations."[15] We use the term "kinship" even though we are talking only about parents and children in this book because in the contemporary United States, the parent-child tie is a cornerstone of kinship.

Taking these two terms together, we define "compulsory kinship" as the taken-for-granted, invisible, yet pervasive set of sociocultural forces that make family of origin relationships—and, for our purposes, *parent-child relationships specifically*—primary, inevitable, natural, and enduring. Pointing out that parent-adult child ties are influenced by the social forces of compulsory kinship—rather than assumed inherent bonds of biology, blood, law, or history—can be met with resistance. Those who have not questioned their intergenerational relationships have a much harder time seeing their parent-adult child ties as at least partly influenced by social forces. But, LGBTQ adults' reflections on their own family of origin life allow us to pull back the curtain, revealing the insidious forces of compulsory kinship.

In the rest of part I, we show why LGBTQ adults adhere to compulsory kinship.[16] Our LGBTQ interviewees use three main framing devices—what we call compulsory kinship rationales—to explain why they maintain their parent-child ties. In chapter 2, we explore the rationale of *love and closeness*, where platitudes of being close to and loving parents are privileged over equally prevalent experiences of strain and discord. Love and closeness rationales were used primarily by white and Asian, cis and trans women, and white gender-expansive people. In chapter 3, we delve into the rationale of *growth*, where LGBTQ people, especially people of color and gender expansive people, emphasize that the promise that parents are becoming more accepting, even if they are still somewhat rejecting, keeps adult children in this relationship. And in chapter 4, we demonstrate the rationale of *uniqueness*, where LGBTQ adults–predominantly people of color—explain they must stay in this relationship because the parent-child tie is irreplaceable, even if it doesn't serve them.

Part II: How LGBTQ Adults Adhere to Compulsory Kinship

Part I shows *why* LGBTQ adults stay in ties with parents through compulsory kinship. Part II explores *how* LGBTQ people stay in difficult relationships with parents. Here, building on the sociological concept of "family work," which refers to a broad number of actions done to promote family functioning,[17] we develop the concept "conflict work" to show how LGBTQ adults do painstaking work to maintain the parent-child tie when there is significant conflict about an LGBTQ identity.[18] In chapter 5, "The Family Closet," we show how white and Asian LGBTQ people enact conflict work by never coming out of the closet to avoid parental rejection. In chapter 6, "Gender and Sexuality School," gender-expansive LGBTQ adults work to make their parents more accepting through education. In chapter 7, "Out of the Closet, Under the Rug," we show how after people across race-ethnicity, gender, and sexuality come out of the closet and unsuccessfully try to educate their parents, they go back "under the rug"—with their LGBTQ identity operating as an open secret. In chapter 8, "Becoming Normal," we show how (only) white cisgender gay and lesbian adults deploy the normative and desirable statuses of married (with children) to get their parents to accept them. Finally, in chapter 9, "Out of the Family," a few LGBTQ people of varying racial-ethnic, sexuality, and gender identities describe parent-adult child estrangement—especially with dads—showing the conditions under which compulsory kinship is rejected.

In the conclusion, we take the position that compulsory kinship perpetuates long-term harm for many adult children. The absence of choice regarding participation in the parent-adult child tie is, as Adrienne Rich says of compulsory heterosexuality, a "great unacknowledged reality." If there is no choice as to whether one remains in a relationship with parents, adult children and their life chances will be at the whim of "chance or luck" regarding the quality of their parents. As such, until staying in relationships with a parent *is* a choice, adult children will "*have no collective power to determine the meaning and place [of parents] in their lives.*"[19] The primacy of parents in adult children's lives can only be obligatory.

The parent-child relationship is so central to the organization and functioning of contemporary society that it is difficult to imagine alternatives. But, in the conclusion, we imagine other ways of organizing society and family life that don't rely as heavily on the parent-child tie financially and in terms of identity and belonging. In doing so, we start to draw a map for how to break free of compulsory kinship. Alternative arrangements for care and community have been suggested by feminist, queer, and Black, Latinx, and Indigenous activists and scholars,[20] often through an "ethics of care" separate from a reliance on parents. We draw on these liberatory ideas to provide us a way out of our reliance (and insistence) on the parent-adult child tie.

While we make a call for change in the conclusion, most of this book focuses on what we see as the reality for most people in the United States today: that parents and adult children are forever bonded. So, while we envision a new way forward at the end of the book, we first need to take stock of the present—where relationships between parents and their adult LGBTQ children are complex, contradictory, and nearly always obligatory.

PART I

Why LGBTQ Adults Stay in the Family

The Power of Compulsory Kinship

1

Compulsory Kinship

Arguably no relationship is longer lasting or more impactful than a child's relationship with their parents. Even as other people and social systems shape children's lives, parents are primary agents of socialization.[1] They teach children how to follow or challenge authority; how to develop economic capacities that are valued in the labor market; and how to negotiate social relationships as gendered, raced, classed, and sexual people in the world.[2]

Even after children become legally independent adults, the importance of parents continues. Very few parents and adult children are estranged—with estimates ranging between 2 and 6 percent of the total population.[3] This rate of estrangement is much lower than the rate for divorce, romantic partner breakups, friendship dissolution, or job termination—pointing to the centrality and continuity of parents for adult kids.[4] Adult kids are intertwined with parents even when their relationship quality is low and conflict is high, as is disproportionately the case with LGBTQ kids and their parents. So why do parent–adult child relationships continue, especially when they're less than ideal? In this chapter, we offer the concept of "compulsory kinship" as an answer to this question.

Remarkably few scholars have tried to chart exactly why the vast majority of parents and adult children stay together. Some scoff at the idea that it would be necessary to understand something so basic and seemingly intrinsic—*we stay in these bonds because they are our parents! It's obvious!*[5] In casual conversation people ask about one another's parents, assuming that adults have ties to them. Parents (and parents-in-law) expect they will spend holidays with their grown kids, and adult children are expected to stay in consistent contact with parents throughout their lives. Parents are supposed to be there, always, to help children with their goals, sometimes serving as "helicopter," "lawnmower," or "snowplow" parents to ensure their adult kids' success.[6] Parents presume that children will get married (to someone of the "opposite" sex) and have children—producing "their" grandchildren—and that their children will care for them when they get older.[7] These are just some of the norms guiding parents and adult children, all of which work to frame the parent-child bond as one that cannot be broken.[8]

We want to question these taken-for-granted expectations and reframe these norms as a part of the operation of compulsory kinship. More on that shortly, but first, we need to provide some background on the parent-child tie with an introduction to how we "do family" today.[9]

Parent-Child Ties and How We "Do Family"

When we take on the title of parent or are given the title of child, we interact with the current corresponding guidelines for how we are *supposed to parent or be a child.*[10] Being a parent or child—and the appropriate behaviors and obligations that come with these labels—is not some "natural" occurrence. Rather, sociologists point out that our broader ideals of what a parent and child should be are informed by historical context, media, local and national governmental policy and law, and local and national culture.[11] It's not that our parental behavior is *completely determined* by society. Rather, we are obligated to adhere to the meaning of being a "good" parent or child through everyday interactions, rewards, and sanctions.

Sociologists call these obligations "normative prescriptive values" (i.e., standards of preferred behavior) enforced in the form of "social norms" (i.e., how things should be done) and "social roles" (i.e., belief in appropriate actions based on social position) that shape how parents and children are supposed to behave.[12] Additionally, there are cultural-cognitive groupings of norms that develop into maps and schemas, which are in turn used to make meaning out of and guide parenthood.[13]

While normative and cultural-cognitive systems are distinct theoretical paradigms and have unique forms, they work in tandem.[14] For simplicity's sake, we refer to these systems together as "sociocultural forces" that inform meanings, expectations, ideologies, values, schemes, and norms that are taken up by everyday people as a way to understand what parents and children are and should be.[15]

Sociologists pay attention to sociocultural forces because they are the scaffolding that guides, shapes, and sometimes controls our behavior. What may at first seem to be individual "choice" is in fact structured by social forces that work to obscure how our individual choices are socially structured and constrained. The very fact that parents and children have their own titles that everyone knows and uses—Dad, Mom, parent, child, son, and daughter—is our first clue that there are powerful sociocultural forces guiding our decisions and behavior. Rather than just a word, these names become shorthand for *who we are—a critical part of our identity*—making it nearly impossible to separate the self from our identities of parent or child.

One way to understand these sociocultural processes is through the concept of "doing family."[16] Doing family draws on the concept of "doing gender," made popular by West and Zimmerman, which refers to how gender is not naturally occurring but instead is enacted in line with the socioloculturally prescribed guides for our behavior and identities.[17] Similarly, in a "doing family" frame, being a parent or a child is not a natural or inherent state but instead is "done" or performed within a sociocultural context in interaction with the self and others. Thus, being a parent or child is the result of "interactional work and activities that create and sustain family ties, define family boundaries, as well as specify appropriate behaviors for different family members."[18]

The "doing family" approach asserts that even though current dominant paradigms privilege biology as a guiding force of identity and behavior,[19] the meaning of parent and child are "achieved and constructed."[20] And the "doing" or constructing of family is done in strong institutional, legal, social, and economic contexts that shape our very ideas of what parents and children should be.[21] For example, one of the primary ways to "do" parenthood is through the emphasis on parental authority over children. Parents' authority over minor children has been taken for granted as natural, inevitable, and immensely powerful, but in fact it is socioculturally prescribed.[22] As D'Emilio writes, "The acceptance of children as dependents, as belonging to parents, is so deeply ingrained that we can scarcely imagine what it would mean to treat them as autonomous human beings," even after children become teenagers and adults.[23] This jurisdiction of parents over "their" children extended not only to what children do (e.g., what school to go to, what to wear, and other activities),[24] but also their physical bodies; parents decide children will undergo surgical procedures, such as circumcision in the case for babies born with penises or genital surgery in the case of intersex children, without consulting the child.[25]

As with gender, people can "redo" what they think of as the ideal parent or child in line with contemporary norms, but we are still constrained within broader sociocultural institutions and interactions that hold us accountable for doing the parent-child tie "correctly." For example, while parents have historically held authority over children, what that authority looks like and how long it lasts has changed drastically over time.[26] It wasn't until the twentieth century that we shifted from framing children as "little adults" who worked alongside parents to a frame of childhood as a novel life course stage of development that required special attention, care, and education. As the family-based economy began to decline due to the rise of industrialization, children went from working on the farm to working in the factory to not working at all—a profound transformation in the meaning and social value of children.[27] Today, having a child is a means of self-realization, identity, and love for parents.[28] As Zelizer puts it, at least as far as parents are concerned children today are "economically useless but emotionally priceless."[29]

How parents "do" parenthood is further shaped by gender, social class, and race-ethnicity. For example, there are prescribed ways to do "fatherhood" and "motherhood," shown in the entrenched gendered labels of the parent role (e.g., mom and dad). What makes a "good" parent strongly differs for mothers and fathers, structured by national and local parental and family leave policies. Motherhood ideals dictate that women are expected to stay home or reduce their work hours to care for their children, while ideals of what it means to be a "good" father have been historically tied to economically providing for children rather than deep emotional ties and childcare.[30] This gendered "doing" of parenthood is further constructed by class. Hays's theory of intensive mothering and Lareau's work on working- and middle-class parents shows there are intersecting gender- and class-specific maps that guide mothering practices; middle-class mothers do "concerted cultivation" by pushing children to participate in school, sports, and extracurriculars, typified by an approach that is "child-centered, expert-guided, emotionally absorbing, labor-intensive, and financially expensive."[31] In contrast, working-class mothers frame children as developing through independent play and "natural growth."

In addition to gender and class, race-ethnicity constrains and shapes parenting behaviors and beliefs in profound ways. Resulting from the legacies of slavery, endemic racism, and xenophobic immigration policy, white children were first and most consistently labeled innocent and in need of protection.[32] To this day, Black, Indigenous, and Latinx children remain regarded as notably *not* innocent, evidenced by the continued adultification of children of color in the US criminal justice and schooling systems.[33] As a result, Black, Latinx, Asian, and Indigenous parents have to contend with racism in order to "do" parenthood. For example, middle-class Black women "redo" mothering through "integrated mothering," which focuses on economic self-reliance, working outside the home, and child-rearing supported by the family and community, as shown in Dawn Dow's book *Mothering While Black* (2019).[34] In turn, in *Essential Dads* (2020), Jennifer Randles shows how Black working-class fathers negotiate the meaning of fatherhood in the context of economic deprivation, racist stereotypes of deadbeat dads, and pervasive expectations of masculinity to create their own version of "hybrid fatherhood."

We could discuss much more on how parenthood is shaped by sexism, classism, and racism, but we simply want to emphasize here that sociocultural ties that bind parents and their young kids are incredibly strong and depend on race-ethnicity, gender, and class.[35]

But what about when kids grow up? Do these sociocultural forces continue, abate, or change? Do parents and adult kids still "do family," and if so, how? We tackle this question next by introducing our concept of compulsory kinship.

Parents and their Adult Kids "Do" Family: Introducing Compulsory Kinship

While many scholars have focused on doing family among parents of young kids, we want to focus on the parent-child tie *after* parents lose their legal control over children at age eighteen. While the *expectation* of intergenerational independence exists in the United States in the twenty-first century,[36] the *reality* is that independence is not the case for most parents and adult children.[37]

Part of the story is that parents and adult kids stay together because kids *need* parents. Economic instability during and following the Great Recession of 2008 and the COVID-19 pandemic, a shortage of well-paying jobs, and the skyrocketing costs of higher education means that today's young adults face diminishing economic prospects, overwhelming job insecurity, increasing debt, a declining social safety net, unequal access to the labor market, and increasing inequality between rich and poor.[38] According to a Pew research report, in 2012, 36 percent of emerging adults (aged eighteen to thirty) spent time living in a parent's household.[39] In 2014, living with a mother became the most common residential arrangement for emerging adults, more so than living with a partner or spouse or living alone.[40] This is in part because young people are more likely to marry and have children (if they do either) later in life than previous cohorts,[41] meaning that their primary social tie remains parents for much longer in adulthood than previous generations.[42] As a result, today's parents are the first and often only line of financial defense.[43]

While financial and practical need is important—especially for people transitioning into adulthood and just getting on their economic feet—it's not the *only* reason why parents and adult kids stay together throughout the life course. While most adult kids do get financial or coresidential help at some point in young adulthood from their parents, most don't rely on their parents substantially for financial help for longer than a couple of years.[44] By the time adult kids exit their twenties, they are mostly financially independent and do not reside with parents.[45] We recognize the deeply tethered financial and practical bonds between adult kids and their parents as part of why this bond stays intact long after children become adults.[46] And, we acknowledge and are indebted to the large body of work showing the importance of finances in keeping young adults and their parents together. But our aim is to focus the rest of this book on something else entirely. That something else is compulsory kinship.

We argue that parent-adult child bonds are maintained not only through financial need but also *through the sociocultural power of compulsory kinship*. We define compulsory kinship as the taken-for-granted, deeply rooted sociocultural expectation that parent-child relationships should be maintained and privileged above most other ties in adulthood.[47] Compulsory kinship involves a pervasive but invisible set of norms and guidelines, similar to the ones mentioned earlier in connection with parent-minor child ties, that frame the parent–adult child tie as natural, normal, and the most acceptable way of being in a family. Maintaining the parent-child tie in adulthood is how we "do" family correctly, and this belief is created, reinforced, and sustained through compulsory kinship.

Adrienne Rich's concept of "compulsory heterosexuality" is key to the development of our compulsory kinship concept.[48] Compulsory heterosexuality is the belief that everyone is and should be heterosexual, enforced through legal and sociocultural structures. This belief, and the organization of society that upholds it, are taken for granted. People assume they (and others) are heterosexual,[49] and deviation from heterosexuality is stigmatized and oppressed. Heterosexuality is then enforced socially (e.g., hate crimes, gay slurs, teaching heterosexist sex education) and legally (e.g., anti-same-sex marriage laws, antisodomy laws, the lack of legal protections for LGBQ workers), making heterosexuality compulsory. Rich shows how women in particular are punished if they do not follow the norms of compulsory heterosexuality and heteronormativity.[50] For women to survive, they must give in to these compulsory forces, keeping in line with the norms of heterosexuality and, in turn, patriarchy—men's social, economic, and political domination over women.

Much like compulsory heterosexuality ensures the primacy of heterosexuality, compulsory kinship ensures the primacy of the parent-child relationship throughout the life course. After we grow up, we could theoretically stop being a "child" and stop having parents.[51] Parents could be something that we have when we are kids but grow out of. But this is not what happens. While compulsory heterosexuality perpetuates patriarchy, compulsory kinship ensures intergenerational hierarchy, or parents' continued power over children. Any other organization of the parent–adult child tie is stigmatized, and as a result, parents and adult children are bound together in what Hess terms a "nonvoluntary relationship." That is, adult kids don't think they have a viable option to leave.[52]

Compulsory kinship draws attention to the fact that we stay in parent–adult child relationships because of deeply embedded expectations and assumptions about how adults should "do" the parent-adult child tie, and because there are serious consequences if one doesn't adhere to these norms. Compulsory kinship is revealed when people stay in these relationships no matter what, framing parents and adult kids as core to the definition of "family" regardless of the quality of their intergenerational tie.

Compulsory Kinship and LGBTQ Adults

We've worked thus far to show that adult relationships with parents are *expected* to stay together forever through the guiding sociocultural forces of compulsory kinship. But now, we turn to our study of compulsory kinship among LGBTQ adults and their parents.

Do LGBTQ kids cut off ties with their parents and get out of compulsory kinship? Are LGBTQ adults and their parents an exception to the rule? The research says, remarkably, no. Even though parents are often rejecting of their LGBTQ kids, and even though LGBTQ kids get less support from parents compared with cishet kids, the vast majority of these bonds persist in adulthood. Most LGBTQ adults see their relationships with their parents as central to their lives—regardless of past and continuing LGBTQ-phobia and rejection.[53]

While of course some LGBTQ kids have supportive parents, a child being LGBTQ is not often taken as good news.[54] Decades of research shows LGBTQ people have more strained and less economically supportive parent-child relationships than cishet people. Parents work hard to assert heterosexuality and gender normativity in their children, and when children do not meet parents' standards, they are often subject to rejection from parents in multiple forms, including expulsion from home and physical and verbal violence, alongside financial withholding and less overall support.[55]

Parental rejection of an LGBTQ kid has significant implications for LGBTQ adults, including higher rates of poverty and being unhoused and worse mental and physical health outcomes relative to cishet people.[56] For example, in *Pray the Gay Away* (2012), Bernadette Barton tells harrowing stories and describes troubling patterns of parental emotional, physical, and financial abuse and rejection toward gay and lesbian children. Gender-expansive people such as transgender and enby folks are at an even *greater* risk of parental conflict, and thus financial instability, due to the heightened stigma of gender nonconformity.[57] While some parents of trans kids are supportive,[58] half of trans youth report either an emotional or a physical break with parents and fear they will be financially deprived or become unhoused.[59] Lowrey and Shepard's *Kicked Out* (2010) provides first-person accounts of young LGBTQ people being kicked out of their homes as a result of their identities, and Brandon Robinson's *Coming Out to the Streets* (2020) shows how being gender expansive exacerbates the risk of becoming unhoused already present for many due to broader systems of economic and racial inequality. Consequences of parental rejection may be felt even more deeply for Black and Latinx people given the interlocking systems of white supremacy, class inequality, transphobia, and homo/bi/queerphobia.[60]

And yet, despite the pain and rejection, almost all LGBTQ adults maintain ties with their parents. In *Invisible Families* (2011), Mignon Moore shows how Black women who love women strategize to keep relationships with unsupportive parents, while in *Queer Kinship and Family Change in Taiwan* (2019), Amy Brainer demonstrates how parents and adult kids alike negotiate their intact ties even after periods of estrangement. Katie Acosta's *Amigas y Amantes* (2013) gives important insights into how sexually nonconforming Latinas sustain and strengthen their relationships with parents, even in the context of forming and sustaining nonheterosexual romantic relationships, and Amy Stone's research demonstrates how adult children reduce parental discomfort with gender and sexuality, keeping this bond intact.[61] One of the inspirations for this book, Kath Weston's *Families We Choose* (1991) shows that even though gays and lesbians form families of choice, this is almost always done while also maintaining (or trying to maintain) their families of origin. Plus, recent studies based on survey data show that LGBTQ people do not report more estrangement with parents than cishet people.[62]

In the context of a wealth of literature that shows LGBTQ adults do adhere to compulsory kinship and stay in often damaging relationships with parents, we need to know more about *how and why* this occurs.[63] Why do LGBTQ adults (and their parents) adhere to compulsory kinship and maintain this relationship? We answer this question in the subsequent chapters in part I. Many of the people we interviewed talked at length about how their parents are damaging, hurtful, disappointing, or in some cases even violent. After we heard these stories, we pushed people to think deeply about *why* they stay in relationships with parents given LGBTQ adults' own characterization of unhealthy parent-adult child dynamics. In interview after interview, their answers show the deep power of compulsory kinship. To explain why they *had* to stay in these bonds and adhere to compulsory kinship, our interviewees deployed the three rationales we'll describe next: love and closeness, parental growth, and parents as unique social ties.

We use the term "rationale" to highlight how people's explanations for their behavior are based in broader sociocultural norms about how to "do" family correctly. These rationales are a way people reconcile what they're *supposed to do* (i.e., compulsory kinship and staying in our parent-child bonds forever, regardless of quality) with perhaps what they might *want* to do or what might be better for them. As such, these three rationales are not just individual-level explanations for behavior. Instead, they arise from deeply patterned sociocultural frames circulating in the United States today that people draw on for how to "do" family. These rationales are a way compulsory kinship is *lived* and *deployed* by LGBTQ adults; they are a way LGBTQ adults themselves justify keeping parents in their lives forever, following the dictates of the current socioculturally dominant model of compulsory kinship.

In chapter 2, we explore our first rationale of compulsory kinship: *love and closeness*. Here, LGBTQ adults offer platitudes of being close to and loving their parents to override ambivalent feelings brought on by parental rejection. In chapter 3, we delve into the rationale of *growth*, showing how LGBTQ adults emphasize that parents are getting better or more accepting, even as parents remain rejecting. And in chapter 4, we illustrate the rationale of *uniqueness*; here, LGBTQ adults explain there is no replacing their parents no matter how bad the relationship is. Thus, this tie has to be forever. Each of these rationales comes from a broader sociocultural frame that makes up compulsory kinship and is drawn upon by our interviewees to explain why they keep their parent-child bonds intact.

The LGBTQ adults we introduce next use the sociocultural rationales of compulsory kinship to "do" family "right," showing that what we think of as individual choices to stay in the parent-adult child tie are in fact deeply prescribed.[64] Their stories provide a glimpse into how compulsory kinship is taken up in people's everyday lives, keeping adult children part of their family of origin forever.

2

The Rationale of Love and Closeness

Sitting in a busy Panera restaurant in the middle of the afternoon on a Thursday, Rin asks Jackie if she has "good" parents. Jackie laughs as she reflects on her fifty-four years of heartache. "I put it this way," she explains. "I was fortunate to have parents that loved me. I was unfortunate to have parents that just couldn't handle it"—the "it" being raising her.

Like so many others whose stories are presented in this book, Jackie, a white trans woman whose sexuality is "evolving,"[1] had a childhood filled with violence and instability that resulted from decades of failed "trickle-down" economic policies and her father's toxic, abusive, and controlling masculinity. As a teenager, Jackie left home due to her dad's abuse. She lived on the street, carrying a toothbrush in her back pocket and staying with her best friend when she could. Sometimes she went camping or spent time in hospital waiting rooms and bus stations. Jackie cried as she told Rin of these tough times, blaming her tears on her being on estrogen. But there is much to cry about in her story. Rin tears up, too, as they sit with the gravity of Jackie's painful childhood.

But what's remarkable about Jackie's story—and that of so many others—is that after all the pain, trauma, disappointment and the years of estrangement, she returns to her parents again and again. Her story is a testament to how strong compulsory kinship really is.

After months on the streets, Jackie moved in with her grandparents, who owned a small farm in Kentucky. Jackie played on the farm, fished, worked tobacco, and milked cows, enjoying the agrarian life in large part because people left her alone. Her two sisters also ran away from home at different points, but they didn't like the farm as much as Jackie did, opting to live with other family members. When Jackie turned eighteen, she joined the military because she didn't know what else to do. Jackie stayed in touch with her mom and two sisters throughout this time, but she didn't talk to her dad for twenty years after leaving home.

When Jackie was thirteen, she realized that she was a girl. But she kept this revelation a secret. After she turned eighteen, she married a straight cis woman and quickly had a child, submerging her childhood discovery. It wasn't until she got out of the Marine Corps that she had even heard of trans people and was shocked to learn "there's more than one." Her exploration took her to the internet, where she learned she could live as a woman. Even so, she felt helpless to change her lot in life. "I was already married, couldn't do nothing about that now. It's like, 'Crap, there's lots of us.'" Jackie felt trapped in her marriage but eventually divorced after several decades. After she divorced, she came out as a gay man, telling both her parents that she's not straight and is HIV-positive. The disclosure did not go well. Now she tries to avoid the subject with her dad, who "gets angry easy." She explains her avoidance, saying, "I change the subject. I want to get along with my dad. If I can't redirect him, then I'll say, 'I gotta go.'" Her mom refuses to discuss her sexuality at all.

Because of these reactions to Jackie's sexuality, she hasn't disclosed her trans identity to her parents and has no plans to do so. "It was hard enough to explain gay to them, much less trans. Who am I to explain trans? I don't understand it." We'll talk more about Jackie not disclosing she's trans in chapter 5, but for now we'll just say she has avoided seeing either of her parents for a year out of fear they will realize she's trans before she's ready to tell them.

Jackie's story is a tug-of-war between the forces of compulsory kinship and her parents' homophobia and (assumed) transphobia. Jackie wants to stay in her family but also is deeply unhappy around them. She lives in this contradiction, saying to her parents, "Go away. I love you. I'll go to hell and back for you, but don't ask to go with me." Jackie is forgiving and kind when talking about her parents, relying on a simple mantra of "You accept people for who they are. You try not to hurt people. You forgive what's the past. . . . At this point, it is what it is."

In the end, Jackie draws on the dominant sociocultural rationale that love *should* be why this tie remains, even when relationships are strained or abusive and evidence of love is absent. "I was fortunate enough to have parents that loved me growing up," Jackie explains. "It's one thing to have a parent that beats you, or physically abuses you," which Jackie's parents did do, "but if they don't love you, that's even worse. . . . Knowing your parents love you, that gives you a little solace."

It doesn't matter if parents treat you poorly, Jackie insists, if there is love. She ends this part of the conversation by drawing on the compulsory kinship rationale of uniqueness (discussed in chapter 4), saying: "If I could choose my family, I wouldn't have chosen them. If they were just my friends, I wouldn't speak to them. . . . With your family, you can't choose your family." The rationale of love will bind them together forever.

Love Is Everywhere

In the modern era, love is *the* organizing principle of family life. While it seems impossible to imagine a time when love wasn't central to family bonds, historians overwhelmingly show that family simply hasn't always been synonymous with love. For most of history, people chose marriage partners (or had partners chosen for them) and had children based on economic survival, pronatalist and heteronormative ideologies, and a lack of birth control, not *primarily* for love. For much of written history, at least in colonial European countries, there was little discussion of parents loving their children or people marrying for love.[2] Through feudalism and the family-based economy in Europe and the colonized Americas, children were rarely discussed in terms of love and affection. Bonds between parents and children were even discouraged due to "fear of becoming attached to a fragile being likely to die young."[3]

It wasn't until the late seventeenth century and early eighteenth century that affection and love were discussed as a characteristic of family life in Europe and by extension in colonized North America.[4] Even then, maternal love during this early era was considered "uncertain, fragile, and imperfect," to say nothing of paternal love.[5] This uncertainty was especially true of enslaved Black parents, whose relationships with their children were controlled by white slave owners.[6]

In the nineteenth and twentieth centuries, love became a *pillar* of the parent-child tie, with children transitioning from "useful to useless."[7] During this era, white children were no longer seen as little workers on the farm or factory but as precious, innocent babes who needed coddling, care, and play.[8] Today, instead of extracting resources from children, children have become avenues of parents' personal satisfaction, with love framed as the primary driver of people's decisions to have children.[9] In turn, love became a dominant sociocultural frame that guides parent–child ties in the United States. As such, love is a key rationale of compulsory kinship.

While this sociocultural rationale of love is a relatively recent historical development, our interviewees consistently use it to explain their persistent parent-adult child ties. Children know they're *expected* to love their parents, and that their parents are expected to love them. This ideal of love, as such, explains the persistent bond. But when LGBTQ adults were asked what love from parents looks like, or how people know they are loved, many were stumped, noting a lack of direct evidence of their parents' love. And, alongside love, almost everyone talked about being "close" to a parent, with closeness often deployed as a pseudonym for love. But as with love, when we asked our interviewees what closeness means or how they know their ties are close, it was clear that their ideal of closeness wasn't always realized.

In using the language of love and closeness to explain a persistent parent-adult child tie, LGBTQ adults provide a glimpse into what is *idealized*, *should be*, or *only sometimes is* the nature of their parent-child tie. We are not doubting that love and closeness are felt; we are not questioning whether this narrative is true. But we are drawing attention to how the ideal of love and closeness is *promoted to obscure conflict, with the goal of adhering to compulsory kinship*. Love and closeness overshadow the darker side of family life to keep the family together. Love conquers all.

"We Love You and We Don't Accept This"

When Clara, a forty-one-year-old white bisexual cis woman, was growing up, she had "an inkling" she liked women. This possibility was too risky to explore, though, because Clara lived with her parents in a religious household. "I was raised Catholic. They're still Catholic," she explains simply, using religiosity as a shorthand for intolerance. But when Clara turned eighteen, she gained further clarity. "I was definitely like, okay, I think I like women . . . and men," and she told her parents. "They just were not okay with the gay thing." Clara tells us, "I might have been twenty or twenty-one and sat them down to have dinner." She cry-laughs as she remembers the moment in all its absurdity: "And they said that was pretty much the worst thing you could have ever told us."

To this day, she's not sure which is worse—her mom telling her she is going to hell and becoming suicidal, or her dad's retreat from the conversation. Clara remembers being particularly upset at the fact that her parents were talking about getting a divorce due to the stress of her being bisexual. "They were so conflicted that they're blaming each other on why I was gay." Clara's older (and only) sister was no help, as she was also biphobic.

This was too much for Clara to bear, and she began living "a double life" to avoid causing her parents more pain. She decided that her sexuality would become "the elephant in the room that we just never talked about." She explains, "I would be gay, have apartments, have girlfriends, you know, we'd live together, and my parents have never seen an apartment I've lived in, ever, until probably this house with [my wife] and I." She notes that this was a great solution for everyone. She "would definitely censor myself around them," and it worked! It seemed like "if they didn't have to deal with it or see it, it was okay." Clara swept her sexuality under the rug to keep the peace, a tactic we discuss in chapter 7.

This under-the-rug approach continued even after Clara dated and then married her wife, Betts. But, after being together for about four years, Betts confronted Clara, saying, "Hey, I should be going home with you and stuff like that." The absence of Clara's family was made even more apparent when Clara would go home with Betts, whose family was more accepting. "It was very nice to have this loving family that really weren't raised with any religion and very open." Clara started thinking to herself, "This is very nice. I do deserve this."

Clara started to bring Betts around more, and it was fine at first. But tensions escalated between Clara and her parents when she told them the pair were trying to get pregnant. Her parents simply said, "You shouldn't do that," to which Clara retorted, "We have the right. We deserve a family too." Painful memories of these conversations emerge in our interview, even after the birth of their child. "I remember on his birth certificate, they said not to use my last name—their last name, which is mine." But Clara didn't listen to her parents. "I did give him my last name. It's hyphenated, just for legal reasons, because I was like, well, fuck them. This is my boy, I put my name on here, 'cause I didn't want to mess around." Clara remembers showing her dad, "and he just kind of looked at it, and I was like, 'Hey, buddy, that's my last name.'"

Things came to a head when Clara and Betts's child was born. "I think they saw him when he was about a week old, and then from there I really was like, 'If you're not with us, you're against us.'" At this ultimatum, Clara's parents finally started to call Clara "mommy," and they have paid attention to their grandson—coming over periodically to visit him. But things aren't perfect. "I think if they were, like, here's a Mother's Day card for the two moms to my son, that would be an optimal situation." Even so, there has been some progress. Clara explains, "Before they weren't calling themselves grandparents to my son, and now it's Granny and Papaw." But, she adds, "I think there's probably still this wish that Betts were a man at the end of the day."

Staying in a relationship with her parents has been a huge struggle for Clara. When asked why she continued the bond through their rejection, Clara responds with the rationale of love. "We just love each other," she explains simply. "It's why we're still in each other's lives." Refocusing the interview on love over conflict allows Clara to continue her parent-child relationship and to justify this decision in her interview. One way she makes this work is by reframing the conflict around her sexuality as a "difference of opinion," rather than disapproval of her identity and life. "I feel like sometimes they think if they agree with that I'm gay or something, they're gonna go to hell." She explains further, "Like, they still have to sometimes throw out there their disapproval." They do sort of accept her, she indicates, even though in the next sentence she also gives us evidence that they don't. And despite their intense lifelong struggle, Clara pivots her assessment, stating, "But on the flip side of it, we were always still sort of close, though." She doubles down on this contradiction a few times in her interview. "And I mean . . . we're close. They would always say 'We love you, we just don't accept this. . . . We love you and we don't accept this.'" Clara knows their so-called closeness and love is tenuous and contradictory. She goes on, saying, "I knew they loved me, I still know they love me, they know I love them." Love is privileged in explaining this continued tie, despite conflict.

For Clara, drawing on the socially sanctioned narratives of love and closeness keeps her in the family—and maintains the parent-child tie at its core—even as it causes Clara and Betts serious pain. She inhabits this contradictory space, one of rejection forever overcome by love, reconciling conflict by emphasizing closeness. Even if Clara's parents don't always act out of love, or act in ways that portray closeness, this relationship is maintained by the rationale of enduring love.

Forgive and Forget

Lucy had it rough growing up in Amish country with three sisters—one younger and two older. A white gay/lesbian GQ/GNC person, the thirty-three-year-old told us of arguments, rejection, and abandonment that peppered her childhood.[10] Lucy's dad was in the military and traveled half the year, and as a result of this distance, her parents married and divorced—twice—and are now remarried to other people. Lucy's mom, Dianna, a fifty-five-year-old white straight cis woman whom we interviewed, struggled with alcoholism while Lucy was growing up. Her parents' problems led to Lucy and her mom becoming unhoused, with Lucy recalling, "I remember being that kid in the car, washing up at a gas station."

When Lucy was seventeen, her mom went to an in-patient alcoholism treatment facility, and her dad moved in with someone he was having an affair with. In turn, Lucy moved in with her older sister. At this point, her relationship with her parents seemed permanently broken due to their negligence, so much so that she didn't even bother telling her parents about her gender and sexuality as she was coming to understand it. Lucy had more pressing concerns: "I had to finish school. I was working a full-time job, going to school, and then we had our own place. Like, I had to lie and say I was eighteen so I could sign a lease. It wasn't legal. My sister was acting as my legal guardian."

Shortly after Lucy's high school graduation, her sister got pregnant, and Lucy followed in her dad's footsteps by joined the military. She noted, "Like, that was it. My sister was pregnant, and I had to go." But not far into her service she was discharged due to what was labeled a mood disorder—a diagnosis she disputes. After hopping from job to job for a while, she went to nursing school, got a good paying job, moved in with her girlfriend, and now considers herself economically secure. Despite her intimate relationship, neither parent has much knowledge about her gender or sexuality, and if they do, they don't talk about it with Lucy. Lucy is firmly in the closet with no sign of coming out (a theme we'll address in chapter 5).

Despite the pain, Lucy looks back on her childhood—and at her parents—through a lens of love. Although she is angry that her dad abandoned her, she also feels sorry for him because he lives with a "lot of regret." Today, she communicates with him once a week on Facebook Messenger and speaks with him once a month on the phone. "He's sorry," she says, explaining why she still talks to him, "I know he is." Even though he is not supportive of her and doesn't know much about her sexuality and gender, she relies on the notion of love to keep this tie intact. "I still love him. And, like, I just talked to him this past week 'cause he messaged me, and he gets weird, and he says, 'I love you.'"

The appraisal of her mom is similar. Lucy knows that her life could have been better, and her bond with her mom more secure if her mom were a more reliable parent. "I know my mom wasn't the best mom, and she could've done better." But, she still privileges love as the primary unifying force because she feels she *needs* to justify the tie's continuation. "I know she's going to die someday, and I know I'll probably feel sorry. . . . I'll feel sad." Why? Because she is her mom, and you only get one mom—a theme we'll address further in Chapter 4. "She's always going to be my mom, and like, I love my mom. . . . My mom, my mom's just, you know, no matter what she's done to me or what she didn't do for me, like, she's always going to be my mom."

Lucy privileges love to keep their bond intact. Relying on the socioculturally endorsed rationale of love allows her to explain the family's persistent bond even in lieu of *evidence* of a supportive and consistent relationship. Lucy keeps both her parents at arm's length with a loving stiff arm. "I'm just kind of by myself for the most part with my family because I love them, but I can only handle so much." Again and again, Lucy does significant work to draw on the ideal of love in her interview, facilitating her ability to keep her parents as a part of her life *no matter what*.

"It's Like We're Close, but Not Close"

A cousin of love is closeness. Much like people use the socioculturally sanctioned narrative of love to explain their persistent parent-child ties, the people we talked to often note, in knee-jerk fashion, that they and their parents are close—and thus forever bonded. But when asked to describe this closeness, these same people articulate they are actually *not* all that close with their parents—or at least this closeness is not entirely evident. This deployment of the ideal of closeness is a key rationale that explains why LGBTQ adults maintain even the most challenging parent-child ties.

Bonnie, a twenty-year-old Korean lesbian/gay/bisexual/queer (LGBQ) cis woman, uses the language of closeness to explain her persistent but troubled bond with her parents. Bonnie is a third-year college student whose parents and younger sister live about thirty minutes from her in her childhood suburb. Bonnie's sexuality has "been something that has been in the back of my mind since literally I was a kid. When I was in middle school, I was really afraid. I went on Yahoo Answers and was like, 'Can I be bisexual?' I don't know what this means." This terrified Bonnie. "I didn't want to be like that. I was like, 'This is abnormal. What's going on?'" She wrote about her questions in her diary, which her mom read. This breach of trust combined with her mom's biphobic reaction created tremendous conflict that still plagues their relationship today. "It was so much trauma that I kind of just blacked it out, almost. Thinking about when she told me that she read through all my stuff, it was very bad. I freaked out. It was really, really, really bad."

Bonnie and her mom haven't directly talked about Bonnie's sexuality since, and neither her sister nor her dad know about her identity—or at least she doesn't think they do. As a result, Bonnie has a very hard time understanding her mom's rejection of her identity in the context of what she frames as an overall close relationship. "It's weird," Bonnie says, "because you would think like, oh, well they're very supportive. They vote for the 'liberal' candidates . . . and they are a very accepting family, vegetarian, all that stuff." And yet, this doesn't translate to an acceptance of her sexuality. Instead, they brush her sexuality under the rug (see chapter 7). "We don't really need to delve into it more," Bonnie says, in part because every time it comes up it causes conflict. As she's gotten older and moved away from home, her self-understanding and love about being LGBQ "just gets easier and better." But she can't talk about these things with her parents.

What does help Bonnie understand her parents' rejection of a nonheterosexual identity is contextualizing her mom as a Korean immigrant. "I mean, obviously, she wants me to have a husband and a family and whatnot," Bonnie explains, drawing on her experiences with Korean conservativism. "She's Korean, so I think she kind of derives from that a more traditional sense of what she wants her child's family to be like." Further drawing on a racial-ethnic explanation for her sexuality being silenced, Bonnie says, "It's just for the Korean people in our family, they don't even know what non-heterosexuality is. . . . It's not even that it's taboo, it's just—it doesn't exist as far as they're concerned. . . . You're going to marry a wealthy man and you're going to be really successful and you're going to live on a golf course or whatever. That's what my mom did."

In her interview, Bonnie tries to make her and her parents seem "close" by framing her mom's cultural heritage as the cause of the family's queerphobia. In doing so, she downplays the contradictory data on a *lack* of closeness. "We're really close," she says matter-of-factly, but then hedges a bit. "I'm close with my family, but it's . . . I don't know." She pauses for a second, thinking through this statement. "We don't really talk about those kinds of things, I guess," a nod to the fact that her sexuality is an off-limits topic. Trying to further explain why she initially described the family as "really close," Bonnie says, a bit sheepishly, "We hang a lot, I guess. I see them a lot. But . . ." Bonnie trails off, finishing her sentence after another pause, noting, "We don't really talk about . . . I don't really like talking about mental illness stuff with them or emotional things or sexuality or just basically anything that I'm uncomfortable with, I guess." Bonnie is even uncomfortable *talking* about talking to her parents about her sexuality.

Bonnie further links closeness to love—what we see as intertwined rationales typifying family ties—saying, "I love them and they're very supportive but they're really. . . . It's too much. I don't like talking to them about personal things because it's very overwhelming and they're just really uncomfortable about it." By her own assessment, there is a strong barrier between Bonnie and her parents that prevents a *total* sense of closeness. Bonnie *is* close to her parents, and they *do* love one another. But in the same breath she notes that closeness and love *should* mean support about her sexuality, which her parents do not provide. The closeness and love are felt but also are overemphasized in her rationale of the tie, in line with the expectation that these relationships are *supposed* to be loving and close. As such, the companion narratives of closeness and love work in service of compulsory kinship, keeping the bond intact.

Bonnie's accounts of her parents—one wherein her parents are close and loving and another with arm's length parents due to their queerphobia—paint a contradictory picture. Ultimately, she privileges closeness over conflict and love over rejection to explain why she stays in the family.

"He Really Loves His Children"

Charlene, a seventy-one-year-old white straight cis woman, and her daughter, Tricia, a fifty-year-old white lesbian cis woman, also draw on the rationale of love as a way to explain their persistent parent-adult child bond. Tricia describes her home life, overwhelmed by her parents' abusive marriage, with anger and deep sadness. "My dad kind of had a rage disorder," she says. "He would punch in walls and he would yell at my mother"—a dynamic her mom confirms in her interview with embarrassment, adding that he also hit her a few times. Tricia and Charlene both stop themselves from giving too much detail, but the effect his abuse had on Tricia is notable when Tricia says, "I'm going to cry if I think about it too much. He was really scary." Charlene tried to leave the marriage several times but was unsuccessful, saying, "I hadn't really been able to make it stick because I didn't have any money." Finally, though, Charlene got herself and Tricia out when Tricia was eleven.

Shortly after the divorce, Tricia's mother got pregnant with a new boyfriend who had moved into their home. Although at first glance this boyfriend appeared kind and fatherly, he repeatedly molested Tricia, then thirteen years old. Charlene only found out about his abuse years later, but their romantic relationship ended for other reasons soon after Charlene's half-brother was born. Without the boyfriend's financial support, Tricia and her mom fell into poverty. Her mom started working two jobs and obtained government assistance, but because her jobs paid minimum wage and the government assistance is minimal, these funding streams barely kept the family afloat. Charlene, who says Tricia "tends to blame me for a million things that were just artifacts of life," resents her daughter for not understand her challenging situation.

Around age fifteen Tricia started to realize that she liked women. She jumped headfirst into lesbian culture, including attending the Michigan Women's Music Festival—a famous festival that catered to women only but was shut down decades later for being trans exclusionary. When asked if she "came out" to her mom at this point, she replies, "I don't know. It was kind of all a part of being political, and rebellious, and growing up. . . . It wasn't like any one point when I came out to my mother." Tricia would simply bring women around and not mention anything about her identity or sexuality.

Because she never officially came out, Tricia doesn't think Charlene believes she is *really* a lesbian. Tricia recounts Charlene saying, "You make things so hard for yourself. Why don't you just go with men." When we talked to Charlene, she confirms this is how she feels, stating, "To be honest with you . . . at bottom, Tricia is really attracted to men." She kept this belief to herself for a while. As she told us, she "didn't say anything like this to her for many years but I did finally. I was bold [enough] to make a comment about it after years of becoming worn out." Charlene was relieved to finally say how she really felt about her daughter's sexuality, but this was a pretty devastating moment for Tricia. Reflecting on this aspect of her relationship with her mom gives Tricia pause. "It's weird," Tricia laments. "It's like we're close, but not close." She goes on to explain this contradiction further, saying, "Even though we're somewhat contentious, I feel like there are certain types of things that only my mother could understand."

In her own interview, Charlene sums up this dynamic by explaining, "As mad as we have gotten at each other over the years for many, many things, and a few times, she's even tried to say, 'Well, I'm just not going to speak to you anymore.' And it always blows over." Even in their darkest times, Charlene tells Tricia, "You're not getting rid of me that easy." Tricia always comes back to her mom, asking for advice and trying to get help with life's everyday calamities. Tricia spends holidays with her mom, they help care for one another when they have health problems, and Tricia gives her mom money whenever she can. In an ideal world, Tricia would want a big, close-knit family, with "all these inside jokes, and this and that and the other, closeness." She ponders to herself, "Why wouldn't I do that with my mother? I don't know. We have much more of a contentious relationship." Adherence to the ideal of closeness and love means that their bonds continue, despite the reality that that closeness isn't really there.

As for her dad, Tricia thinks she *also* needs to maintain this injured tie. When she sees him once every few months, it's not enjoyable because "you can't argue with him, and he gets really mad." But Tricia says she stays in touch with him because "he doesn't really have any other [people]." She even goes as far to say, "He's going to weaken and eventually die and I'm going to be there. I'm the only one there, really." In her interview, Charlene draws on the rationale of love to explain this bond, saying, "See, one thing about [him] is he really loves his children, even if they don't want to speak to him, even if they hate his guts . . . he really loved his children." Tricia and her dad maintain their bond through the narrative of love as well as the notion of "uniqueness" that is discussed in chapter 4.

Tricia simply does not have the relationship with her mom or dad that she wants. Instead, the triad share the liminal place between love and pain, staying together due to compulsory kinship and explaining their bond through the ideal of love and closeness.

Conclusion: What Is Love?

Love and closeness are the current ideal of what is *supposed* to guide our most important relationships, including those with our parents. But many relationships are more complex than this ideal. In this chapter, we have shown how LGBTQ adults remain in relationships with parents—something they feel they *should* do due to compulsory kinship—by privileging closeness and love over conflict and tension. The rationales of closeness and love work in the service of compulsory kinship, giving adults and their parents the language to justify their intact but imperfect ties. These rationales keep the parent-child bond together, despite the fact that some LGBTQ people may be better off without this compulsory bond.

Notably, few men (trans or cis) deployed this rationale. Those inhabiting masculinity as a primary identity may not want to engage in love and closeness talk—or use this language as a way to explain their persistent parent-child ties—due to stigma about femininized emotions.[11] Perhaps those identifying as women, GQ, GNC, or enby more routinely relate to others through discourses of love and intimacy and thus use notions of love and closeness more regularly to explain their persistent relationships. Further, white and Asian people in our sample used love and closeness to explain their persistent relationships to parents, while few Black, Latinx, or Indigenous people we talked to deployed this rationale. This does not mean that Black, Latinx, or Indigenous people never discuss love or closeness in family life, but rather that white and Asian people seem to be more focused on using the ideals of love and closeness to justify their persistent family bonds. This may be due to structural or cultural differences in how parent-adult child ties are perceived and managed across racial-ethnic groups and also may reflect our specific sample of interviewees, which we reflect on further in the appendix.

Many people think about closeness and love as the basis of our most important family relationships. But the *ideal* of closeness and love is often not fully realized. Rather, "love" and "closeness" in the abstract are used as a justification for maintaining the parent-adult child tie in service of compulsory kinship.

3

The Rationale of Growth

Alicia, a forty-one-year-old Native American bisexual trans woman, has a rocky relationship with her mom.[1] Her biological dad was never in the picture—Alicia "has no clue who he is"—leaving Alicia's mom alone to raise her. Her mom struggled with substance use and mental health issues that disproportionally plague people of Indigenous descent due to the long-lasting impact of economic and social disenfranchisement.[2] As a result, Alicia went into foster care at the age of eight and remained there until eighteen.

Alicia tried to undergo gender transition during her years under the guardianship of the state but was consistently rebuked by social workers, school therapists, and foster parents. "It was very tough because I was so wanting to be feminine, but every time I tried I was shot down," she recalls. Due to social pressures and an attempt to be accepted by her foster families, Alicia "went full-bore masculine," getting involved in sports and acting and dressing masculine. This approach took a profound toll on her soul. Alicia explains, "So I was never happy. And in a lot of my pictures looking back, the ones I still have, I was never happy. There's never a smile. There's always, at worst, I want to say lifelessness in the eyes. At best anger." This unhappiness resulted in several suicide attempts and stays in treatment facilitates, which Alicia says never helped. "I just, kind of like a quiet church mouse, suffered in silence, was miserable," she explains, simply. "I never had that opportunity to fully be myself."

Alicia and her mom reconnected when Alicia was sixteen, and Alicia came out to her mom as bisexual soon thereafter. She explains, "When I came out to my mom, it wasn't that I was trans at first, it was that I was bisexual because I had identified as bi or gay from a young age and she had kind of had an inkling. But I confirmed at least that much to her." Her mom didn't care all that much about this revelation—at least not outwardly. Alicia moved back in with her mom when she was eighteen after leaving the custody of the state, in part to help raise her sister as a "de facto second parent."

While Alicia's mom seemed fine with her being bi, she did not accept her being trans. "When I first came out as trans, I think I lost her," Alicia says of her coming out in her midtwenties. "She got kind of distant with me." Her mom could simply not handle Alicia's gender transition and started to disassociate from her. Alicia had lost her mom before and was worried she would again. "We were kind of tight, and then we fell apart," she says with remorse. But the relationship did not completely sever due to the power of compulsory kinship. Today, Alicia paints the picture of their relationship through the lens of growth. While her mom is "not knowledgeable to this day," still telling Alicia, "I don't understand it. I don't know if I'll ever fully understand it," Alicia takes what she can get. "At least it's not like some people out there," she says, "whose parents completely disown them. So I am grateful for that."

The bar isn't high, and Alicia's mom often still can't reach it. Alicia says, "She still calls me 'son' on the phone, and I still have to correct her much to her chagrin. And sometimes—she'll do good, she'll do good, she'll do good, and then she'll slip up." Alicia takes this misgendering in stride. "Because every time she does it . . . I do a face palm and it's like, 'Oy.' And it's like, 'No mom. I'm not your son anymore. I'm your daughter.'" To this, Alicia's mom replies, "I'm sorry, son. I mean, daughter."

Despite this constant misgendering, Alicia is forgiving. "I think she's genuinely trying," she explains, "because when I correct her, she seems a little hurt." The fact that her mom is *trying* to do better, even though she consistently misgenders Alicia, is what's important. Alicia chooses to focus on those parts of her mom that have grown and are growing still, rather than the parts of her mom that are transphobic.

One way Alicia has facilitated this growth is asking for her mom's help in choosing a name. "I knew what I wanted my name to be," she explains, "but I wasn't sure about the middle name, and the spelling of it I wasn't quite sure. I included her in that process. Including her in that almost seemed to make her accept me more." Alicia focuses on this growth as she works to keep the relationship together.

Alicia's relationship with her mom is improving, but this progress is happening in the broader context of confusion, tension, strain, and continued misgendering. Alicia's mom is better than so many other parents, she thinks, and her mom's low-key efforts are a huge deal to Alicia. Alicia works to highlight any growth to keep them bonded rather than focusing on the transphobia that pushes them apart.

It's Getting Better All the Time

Much like in chapter 2, which describes LGBTQ adults who draw on the current sociocultural norms of love and closeness to adhere to compulsory kinship, the LGBTQ people portrayed in this chapter use the rationale of progress to explain their persistent parent-adult child bonds. Alicia's emphasis on parental growth mirrors the broader ethos embraced by the gay rights social movement in the late twentieth and early twenty-first century: "It Gets Better." This phrase emerged out of the "It Gets Better" project, launched in September 2011 by white gay celebrity Dan Savage, a cis man, and his husband, Terry Miller.[3] Aimed at LGBTQ teens who face bullying from their peers or rejection from their parents, Savage and others—including comedians Ellen DeGeneres, Margaret Cho, and Neil Patrick Harris, and celebrities such as Lady Gaga, Adam Lambert, and George Takei—spoke directly to LGBTQ teens to tell them that life gets better after high school. These good-looking and rich gay celebrities, the project asserts, give hope to troubled teens that a brighter future exists.

But critics argue that "It Gets Better" relies on a flawed and unrealistic sexual liberation progress narrative. In the *History of Sexuality Volume I: An Introduction*, Foucault argues that the belief that we are always progressing toward sexual liberation is ahistorical.[4] We haven't, in fact, always been moving toward increased sexual liberation. Instead, what the record shows is a constant back-and-forth between tolerance and repression of those sexualities and genders outside the cishet norm. But the promise of the future is appealing—in popular culture and in the minds of our interviewees—as a way to take a bad situation and make it livable.

Interviewees craft their *own* stories of progress—of it getting better—in the context of this broader cultural progress narrative to make sense of their persistent relationships with parents. For those portrayed in this chapter, parents are often highly problematic and hurtful but are simultaneously framed as *better today than ever before* and thus *on the linear path to "better."* Parents are *trying* to get better, allowing children to stay in relationships despite sometimes overwhelming evidence that progress is not exactly monumental. As with the rationale of love and closeness, we're not questioning whether parents actually are getting better as some objective truth. Instead, we point to how LGBTQ adults privilege *any* amount of progress—what Sara Ahmed (2010) might call the "promise of progress" to remain bonded to parents and to keep in line with compulsory kinship. These progress stories are a way people frame themselves and their parents to give hope during dark times.

"At Least She's Trying"

Jamie doesn't like to talk about their childhood, and for good reason. Jamie's parents "were very emotionally and mentally abusive to each other." If that weren't enough, "sometimes it would be physical abuse and sometimes I would be dragged into it as a kid." This abuse led to their parents divorcing when Jamie was seventeen, an event Jamie knew "was just a matter of time." Since then, Jamie has had a continued relationship with their mom, who remarried. Jamie's dad was incarcerated when they were young and has been in the background of the family portrait ever since.

Despite having had a really difficult childhood, Jamie, a Black and Asian twenty-two-year-old trans/GQ/GNC person who identifies as sexually queer, moves forward by privileging growth and de-emphasizing conflict to explain the persistence of their parent-child tie. Jamie's mom knows about their queer sexual identity but not their trans/GQ/GNC identity. "We haven't had like a full-on conversation about it," Jamie explains, in part because they want to avoid the inevitable conflict that comes with explaining their gender. Because parents so often misgender their gender-expansive kids by using incorrect pronouns or a "deadname," Jamie is worried about disclosing.[5] Jamie is just not sure how their mom will respond to this news, but has hope that she will learn to accept them.

Jamie has a bit of evidence that their mom *might* be supportive based on one recent interaction. Jamie's mom is moving to the Southwest and asked Jamie to come too. Jamie didn't want to go but had a hard time explaining why. "I found out specifically that there is not a large queer community there and that the LGBT community mostly caters to only cis white gay men." Their mom did not understand what the problem was. "She didn't understand it. Because I told her that there was not much of a community and she was like, 'There's lots of gay people here, I've seen lots of gay men.' And I'm just like, 'That's not the same mom.' And she was like, 'Well the girl at my job is gay,' and I'm like, 'That's not the same either.'" Jamie hinted at their gender identity in this conversation, but stopped short of fully explaining themself. Jamie sighs with frustration but is also filled with hope because at least their mom is open to learning. "She was just like 'Okay, well, you'll have to explain this to me later. . . .' She's trying, which is a thing that I appreciate at least is that she's trying to understand at least."

Jamie takes their mom's effort as a sign that the bond is worth keeping. "I mean, now I feel a lot closer to mom than ever before because I've been having more discussion with her about myself and things that I'm going through," Jamie explains. Their mom is *finally* showing signs of being able to listen. "I talked to her more about it, and she's lot more supportive of the things that I do." This growth mindset keeps them bonded, despite their past, with the promise of even more growth to come.

Jamie's dad is another story. Jamie recently told their dad about their sexuality and hinted at their gender, and this disclosure did not go well. "I first told him, kind of, um . . ." Jamie stops midthought to explain their dad's personality for context. "When I speak to my dad, it's more of, like, I get one sentence of my point I want to get across, and then he like butts in and he like berates the one sentence before the hears the rest of the point." As a result, Jamie never really got to discuss their identity with their dad. But regardless of this not-so-great "conversation" and overall challenging relationship, Jamie emphasizes that their dad is in fact, too, getting better all the time. "He's posted stuff on his Facebook that have been like transphobic and things like that," they explain, "so I've like posted on it and I've told him like why it's wrong and like it's very terrible that like he feels this way, especially when his own child is this way." In response, "I think he ended up deleting the whole post." Jamie sees this as progress—as hope of a better future with their father.

Jamie's parents' recent change in behavior and attitude—even just the promise of change—doesn't erase past pain or alter the fear of future rejection. But the framing of their parents as growing allows Jamie to put a positive spin on their relationships. Jamie doesn't really know whether their parents are going to become more understanding and supportive over time. But despite all the pain, the hope of growth provides the tools to explain the intact, albeit problematic, relationships today.

"Whatever . . . He's Getting Better"

Brian is a thirty-six-year-old white straight trans man who also draws on the narrative of growth to explain his persistent, albeit troubled, relationship with his dad. Growing up, Brian lived with his twin sister and his mom and dad. Brian remembers being "very, very quiet growing up.

I was the kid that could sit in a class for an entire year and not say a word to anybody." Brian was very close with his sister and remembered their parents giving them "lots of leeway to do our own thing" when they were growing up. Brian's mom passed away from cancer in 2008—before he could tell her about his gender identity—but Brian's dad is alive and a plane ride away; the twins go to see him every year at Christmas.

Brian came out to his dad as a lesbian in his early twenties "before I knew that trans was even a thing." His dad later found out Brian was trans when his sister outed him ten years later. The reaction was not good. "If you ask my dad, he says that he was with it right away," Brian says. "No. He was not." Brain's dad took a stonewalling approach to his son being trans. As Brian recalls, "It was one of those things we just didn't talk about. Bring it up, he'd change the subject." This approach fits with their overall relationship dynamic. "He and I don't really talk about stuff. We tell funny stories, he tells me what's going on in his neighborhood, I tell him what's going on at work. We don't have conversations about stuff. I think that's how it's always been."

However, not talking about Brian being trans is challenging, especially when Brain and his sister went to see his dad for a visit for the first time after Brian was outed by his sister. "I don't think he even got the name or pronoun right the whole time I was there," Brian laments. But once Brian started testosterone and was able to start physically embodying how he felt internally, he saw a shift in his dad. "When I went back a few months later at Christmas, my voice was a little bit deeper and then, maybe once a day he got the name and pronoun right."

Bit by bit, Brian feels his dad was getting better. To hasten the transitions of both his body and his dad's acceptance, Brian's dad helped him pay for his recent top surgery. "Dad did loan me the money for [the surgery], which was cool," he says in disbelief. "I didn't think he was going to. I was going to take out a loan." But to Brian's surprise, his dad told him, "Well that's ridiculous. I'll just loan you the money and you pay me." This was a major step toward acceptance. "I didn't ask, he just offered, which was cool."

Now, after top surgery and time on testosterone, Brian classifies his body as "mostly passing," and as a result, he has seen a change in his dad. "I think we're up to a couple times a day now, he gets the names and pronouns right," Brian says flatly—both happy but also not impressed. Brian explains that his dad thinks he's doing really well with correctly gendering him, but "I want to be like, 'Not really.'" Still, Brian doesn't try to push his dad because his dad doesn't respond well. "Any time I give him a hard time about it, he'll be like, 'I'm doing a pretty good job, I think. I'm trying.' I was like, 'Okay . . . ?'" Again, Brian doesn't agree that his dad is doing a good job but is willing to give his dad a pass. As shown in other work on transitioning, the more Brian looks like he passes as fitting within a Western sex/gender binary system, the better his dad gets at correctly gendering him.[6] "The joke is I'm going to come home one time with a beard and then maybe he'll be better about it, if I can grow a damn beard."

Despite some lamenting, Brian ends his conversation with Rin on an upbeat note emphasizing the narrative of growth about his dad's use of the correct pronouns. "Yeah, I mean, he's getting better. He does better, he doesn't say 'the girls' anymore, most of the time, which is nice. He still calls me [deadname] sometimes, which, whatever . . . he's getting better." In the same sentence, Brian notes how his dad is still failing, but also that he's getting better. Brian mentions how his dad sometimes still calls his children "the girls," occasionally deadnames him, or sometimes uses the wrong pronouns—all of which are true. But, then, he presses a positive spin. By showing how far his dad has come, Brian overpowers the negative and reframes the future—all in service of compulsory kinship.

The Promise of the Future

Morgan, a thirty-nine-year-old Chinese and white gay, lesbian, queer cis woman, sees the future as getting better all the time—at least when it comes to her mom's homophobia and gender policing. Morgan's biological dad passed away when she was a baby; Cameron, a sixty-three-year-old white straight cis man who she and her brother call dad, was a family friend who eventually married her mom. Morgan has always been "very close" to Cameron, noting, "He was the first person, back in the late nineties, early 2000s, that identified my homosexuality and just gave me comfortable and good opportunities to come out. Never pushed me, but he was the one I first came out to." Morgan and her stepdad get along "famously," according to Cameron, much more so than Morgan and her mom, Christine.

While Cameron has been nothing but supportive of Morgan's sexuality, telling Morgan, "Hey, it's okay if you're gay," Morgan and Christine really didn't talk about Morgan's sexuality until recently. "On one level it was a little harder for her to accept," Cameron explains. "I think [Christine] was kind of in denial about it at first." Morgan ties this denial to her mom being Chinese: "My mom has Chinese cultural influences, so we don't really talk about a lot. It's more indirect." Comparing Cameron and Christine against one another, Morgan continues, "We didn't talk like I did with my stepfather . . . and I think it's just more cultural norms that kept us from having a direct conversation." At one point in Morgan's childhood, this lack of direct conversation and consistent tension came to a head when Christine kicked Morgan out of the house for disobeying her rules regarding sexuality. Morgan then spent six months living with another family when she was a teen.

Morgan has had other more recent conflicts with her mom about her sexuality, but she emphasizes that things have gotten better and better over time. Importantly, her mom has "stopped pressuring me to present in a more feminine appearance," which has lifted a great weight off of Morgan's shoulders. And, surprising everyone, "She's talked more directly about LGBT issues and most recently, she actually went to the pride parade." Cameron also talks about Christine's growth. "Well, at some point we started talking about it more, and I think she just realized that Morgan was still the Morgan we always knew, and that she really wasn't different because of her sexual preferences," Cameron explains. "I think Christine just came to that realization." Morgan has also noticed an overall change, more of an "I support you and who you are" approach. But, much to Morgan's annoyance, her mom still uses "feminine words for beauty . . . you know, 'You are beautiful, you are pretty.'" This is not how Morgan would like to be talked about, but she's started to accept that this is part of their relationship.

Morgan focuses on the growth of her mom, explaining that it is due to "time and maybe more societal acceptance. Her colleague that she co-owned a business with has a gay daughter as well, who's out. I think that may have helped in having support with someone that she works closely with and socializes with. They both have LGBT children." Morgan believes that increasing societal LGBTQ acceptance has helped her mom grow, and this growth helps keep the relationship intact and functioning, even as Morgan's gender and sexuality are muted.

Despite her emphasizing growth, at the end of her interview Morgan brings up again how she thinks her mom's racial-ethnic identity shapes her lack of full acceptance. "One Chinese trait is that we tend to kind of scoop things under the rug," she says. "I would like to be more open and talk about more things. Like maybe, for example, when my mom was pressuring me or expressing her desire to present a more feminine appearance, I would just kind of brush it off, but I could have talked to her more directly about it. I wish I could do it even more directly." Morgan's relationship with her mom certainly isn't perfect, but she keeps this tie in line with compulsory kinship because there's enough progress to allow her to assert that it's getting better.

Conclusion: Families Getting Better

LGBTQ adults maintain their parent-child ties in accordance with compulsory kinship despite having parents who are often highly hurtful at worst and not fully understanding at best. One way LGBTQ people explain their persistent parent-child tie is by leveraging evidence of, and hope for, growth. Parents are *always getting better*, so the relationship can continue, even if it is still deeply conflictual.

In this chapter, we saw the rationale of growth being used more obviously and with stronger emphasis by people of color and gender-expansive people. People of color—in this chapter Asian, Indigenous, and Black people—have particular racial-ethnic experiences that make gender and sexuality a site of strain. For example Asian traditionalism is called out by interviewees as a source of homophobia and transphobia, and the legacies of settler colonialism, which imposed Western gender binaries and the white colonial surveillance state, structure the parent-child relationships of the LGBTQ folks of color we talked to.[7] This chapter shows that the dynamics of queer, gay, bi, and transphobias are specific to each racial-ethnic sociohistorical location, as are the specific ways parents become more accepting. As such, people of different racial-ethnic identities draw on distinctive characteristics and behaviors to evidence parental growth.

Moreover, the gender-expansive people in this chapter reveal a uniquely challenging parent-child dynamic to work through. Given that their gender nonconformity cannot easily be hidden, and given that far less social progress has been made regarding gender-expansive identities relative to nonheterosexual sexualities, gender-expansive people often face parents who haven't even *heard* of their identities. This in turn means that most parents have a lot of growing to do, with any possible effort toward that growth, no matter how inconsistent, seen as progress. We'll discuss why gender-expansive people often deploy the narrative of growth to stay in the family through educational work, and how this helps preserve the parent-child tie, more fully in chapter 6.

In this chapter, parents are *reframed as always becoming* more supportive; this growth is a rationale explaining why LGBTQ people can maintain the current norms of family with the parent-adult child tie intact. Many parents *have* gotten more accepting of their child's LGBTQ identities. But, the promise of progress (Ahmed, 2010) obscures the pain of the past and present. The rationale of growth is a key dimension of compulsory kinship that keeps LGBTQ kids bound to parents. Hope springs eternal, even as rejection remains.

4

The Rationale of Uniqueness

Gordon is a matter-of-fact nineteen-year-old Black queer trans man whose family life has been nowhere near ideal. Gordon was adopted as a newborn by a white couple who subsequently divorced when he was two. His mom remarried quickly after the divorce to a man who abused both her and Gordon. Both of his father-figures died when Gordon was seven; his adopted dad of cancer and his stepdad by suicide, which Gordon witnessed. From then on, he and his mom moved across the country, living in a dozen different states. Gordon laughs when he remembers that all this moving meant he never learned the concept of slopes in math class. "Like, when I was in middle school, we'd start on slopes, we'd move. I remember in sixth grade, we were in Florida, and my teacher was like, 'We're gonna do slopes today,' I was like, damn. That means we're moving. And a week later we moved."

Gordon's mom, a white straight cisgender woman, ran out of money and settled in the Midwest, where her siblings live. Gordon explains that they moved to a white suburb in order to stay away from the Black community, which his mom deems "dangerous." Gordon is hurt and perplexed by his mom's racism, saying, "She's just spooked by them, I don't know why. But she just acts like she didn't adopt a [Black] child. I didn't really understand." He just responded with "Okay mom" because "we're stuck together." The constant moving and his mom's unstable mental health created severe precarity for Gordon throughout his young life. During his last two years of high school, he and his mom were living out of her car. "She wasn't very big on keeping a job," he explains, "and then I had to drop out of school so I could work full-time and take care of her."

Gordon came out to his mom as queer about five years ago and as trans about a year ago. At the start, Gordon loved telling people his mom was supportive. But, after six months, "something happened and she snapped," Gordon explains, "and I don't even know what it was. But all of a sudden, she was like, that's not good." From then on, his mom simply didn't accept his trans status, creating more instability in their already volatile relationship. "She was like, 'You can't transition, it's bad, it's just all bad,'" Gordon says. "She was under the impression God made you perfectly the way you are, so you don't need to transition." But this didn't stop Gordon. "And I was like, sure, but I'm gonna do it anyway. I feel this way, I'm gonna go with it."

Gordon felt he could not be himself around his mom. But they were stuck together—at least until he turned eighteen. "I couldn't just do things on my own. And she had the car, and I didn't have a driver's license. And I couldn't really stay anywhere, like with other people, until I was eighteen, because I had to have her permission basically." Gordon's dependence on his mom was the driving force in their staying together. "To avoid being actually out on the street, it was like, 'Well, at least we have this car roof over our heads.' And I didn't want to ruin that bit. That's why I put up with most of her stuff, 'cause we were stuck together." As a minor, Gordon felt trapped by the legal and financial bonds.

Like so many others we talked to, Gordon views his mom's lack of acceptance as stemming from her religious upbringing, explaining, "Yeah, that's my southern mom for you. . . . She was just really religious, and the whole transgender thing was not her cup of tea." This is a common refrain, as religion plays a key role in the rationales of parental homophobia or transphobia in the United States today.[1] But about six months ago, after Gordon turned eighteen, he sensed a shift in possibilities. While the two were living in an extended stay motel room, they had a fight about Gordon being trans. Gordon called the police because his mom was threatening to harm him and herself. She was taken to the hospital for psychiatric care, and the two went their separate ways afterward. "At the time, because I was working, I just Ubered to a different hotel and didn't tell her until I could find an apartment or somewhere to stay. That was our separation." Gordon was excited about his newfound independence. He had a steady job and was able to pay for his week-by-week space on his own for the first time ever. He didn't need his mom to care for him financially, and legally he was finally independent.

Today, Gordon lives on his own, while his mom is unhoused in a nearby suburb. Did he cut his mom off after he didn't need her financial help? He thought about it, that's for sure. He won't live with her again, but surprising even himself, he hasn't cut his mom out of his life. Despite all the strain and conflict, Gordon doesn't stop answering his mom's calls. Why? He would like to never talk to or see her again, and legally and financially he doesn't *have* to. But when push comes to shove, Gordon can't let go of this relationship; the two remain connected because *he sees it as his unique duty as her only child*. "She's my mom," he simply says.

No one else can take his place in the family, nor hers. He holds out hope that she'll be able to have a relationship with him that is mutual and respectful, but he will remain in touch with her regardless. He is forever obligated to her by virtue of being her kid, as he believes there is no way to "do" family without his mom.

Once a Child, Always a Child

Why does Gordon remain in a relationship with his mom? Gordon certainly doesn't see he and his mom as close in the normative sense, and in his interview Gordon could not even say that he loves his mom or that she loves him. Nor does he see his relationship with his mom getting better over time. Gordon doesn't even need his mom for financial help any longer. And yet, he can't let the relationship go. When nothing serves as a logical explanation for this persistent tie, a final dominant socioculturally endorsed rationale prevails: the rationale of uniqueness.

Compulsory kinship involves the belief that the parent-child tie is always at the center of the family. Even when most of the expectations for the quality and form a parent-adult child tie should take—such as loving, close, or growing—are not realized, adults don't abandon their parents. Why not? Because compulsory kinship tells us there is *no other bond that could ever replace that between parent and child.* Like the other two rationales of love and closeness and growth, the rationale of uniqueness emerges from broader sociocultural forces that inform the right way to "do" family through compulsory kinship. To manage the societal expectation to stay in relationships with parents no matter what, the people we talked to enforce upon themselves the basic assumption that parents (and children) are *irreplaceable, unique, and involuntary.* This framing is built around current assumptions of genetics, blood, legality, history, and a shared long-standing relationship that links parents and children together, forever.[2]

There is no law obligating adults to their parents, no rule saying those who birthed, adopted, or raised a child must take a central position in their family. And yet, even when parents fail to keep their end of the bargain by being unsupportive and even deeply damaging, the prominent belief is parents must remain in the family. "Parent" and "child" are the core of how we do family, with unique obligations forever. Till death do you part, for better or worse.

"Mom Gets a Pass"

Natalie, a forty-six-year-old Black trans GQ/GNC woman who identifies as straight, bisexual, gay, lesbian, queer, and pansexual, was born into a military family in the South.[3] She and her mom stayed in the US while her dad lived abroad for months at a time. She describes having had a loving home with a mom was who was "always available" but a dad who was uninvolved and disinvested.

Natalie knew early on that she wasn't like other people of her sex and gender assigned at birth. "At about age twelve, I figured out that something was kinda wrong, or different. I hate the word wrong, but something was different." She didn't feel able to explore her so-called difference in her home environment, so "I tried to suppress it, and move forward with life." Her desire to hide her gender well into adulthood—

even from herself—was reinforced by a terrible encounter with her mom as a teen. When Natalie was fourteen or fifteen, her mom changed her bedsheets and found undergarments underneath the mattress. Natalie's mom confronted her about it, asking, "Why do I have her stuff? Do I want to be a girl? Am I gay?" Natalie denied these correct statements. "I was so petrified that I didn't know how to respond. I just said, 'No, no, no,' to everything . . . even though I had so much more to say. Then she spanked me." Natalie pauses to correct herself, saying, "I'm not gonna say spanked me. She gave me a whoopin' out of this world. At that point I knew that I couldn't really talk about how I felt." This moment is forever stuck in Natalie's memory as traumatic, leading her to ignore her gender identity until much later in life. "I just bottled it up and kept it to myself."

After this encounter, Natalie fully embraced what she thought would be perceived as masculinity. "I did scouting. I played basketball. I went to college. Pledged a Black fraternity, and did all of the things that one would consider very male-type of activities." While things were good, "I was faking the funk in terms of gender. I just didn't know I was faking the funk. I mean, everything was cool. I mean it was cool, other than me faking the funk." This approach to gender continued after college, when she married a cisgender woman and had a child.

It wasn't until Natalie turned forty that she began to come to terms with her gender. Natalie divorced her wife and told her mom she was trans. This disclosure did not go well, and things haven't gotten much better since. At the time of our interview, Natalie's mom still doesn't treat her the way she wants to be treated, constantly misgendering her. "My mother's very religious," Natalie explains. "She comes from a Black Baptist background, so she always was like, 'Have you prayed?'" Natalie's dad was diagnosed with a combination of Alzheimer's, dementia, and Parkinson's, and thus "he's really not a player in the equation, because for all intents and purposes he is, unaware if you will."

Things with her mom haven't improved over time, and the two still struggle to have a relationship. Yet, despite this long-standing tension and continued lack of support, Natalie has stayed connected with her mom. How does she explain this? "I don't get upset about it. That's my mom. She put me on this earth, and I'm not gonna fight her about that given everything else that she has going on with my dad, and her age, and the whole nine yards. It's not worth the fight." While it's frustrating, she is willing to forgive her mom for the rejection and continued misgendering because "Mom gets a pass, you know?" She says it again, as if to double down, "Mom gets a pass." This is the case even when her mom "yells out that deadname to get my attention." When this happens, Natalie will answer, but "it is frustrating because I hear this, and that's not what I want to be addressed by, but *it's my mom*."

Natalie's mom is placed in a special category of people. "She gave birth to me. She put me on this earth, you know?" Because of the gift of life, Natalie's mom is special, irreplaceable, and deserving of a pass, no matter what. For Natalie, the conflict around gender and sexuality is no match for the deep-seated uniqueness bestowed upon the parent-child bond. This relationship isn't ordinary, it is extraordinary, and "doing" family correctly for Natalie means that this bond *will* be forever. Due to compulsory kinship, Natalie can't even imagine a world that doesn't involve her mom, even if she's not the mom Natalie wants.

"You Only Get One Mom"

Cheryl is a twenty-eight-year-old Black gay/lesbian person who identifies as both a man and a woman but is known solely as a woman to her family of origin. Cheryl lived with her mom throughout her childhood, but she moved out at seventeen when her mom found out she was a lesbian. During this outing encounter, Cheryl's mom threatened to call the police after finding Cheryl and her girlfriend together in her room. "She said I was going to hell. I'm nasty. My mom hit the fan." Cheryl went to live with a friend, then lived with her girlfriend for a few months. After the pair broke up, Cheryl stayed with another friend for a period and eventually went to live with her dad.

Cheryl and her dad got along well, with him even expressing support for her sexuality and gender. "My mom always wanted a little girl she could dress up, and my dad knew that something wasn't right on that front. And I always wanted to wear boys clothing and fight with the boys, and my dad he always just took it for what it was." Despite his support, her dad's house wasn't stable because she and her stepmom, who also lived there, often argued. "She was bipolar," Cheryl explains, "and I'm headstrong." This led to Cheryl's stepmom periodically kicking her out of the house, leaving Cheryl to fend for herself on the street, with a friend, with her aunt, in a car, or with a lover. "Like, I would say, 'Hey, can I stay the night here?' If it was a big issue or if it was a 'no,' I'd just move on to the next person." Finally, her grandmother provided stable housing for a couple of years, allowing Cheryl to get a job and enroll in community college.

Despite the rejection, Cheryl has recently begun to reconnect with her mother. When Rin asks why she choose to reconnect after the pain her mom has caused her, Cheryl deploys a rationale of uniqueness:

> *You only get one.* When my stepmother passed I watched my brother. Before she passed away, they would get into it. He would cuss her out, scream at her, yell at her. He just has so much regret and guilt with him now. It's just, like, I don't want that. You only get one parent, so it's better to just move past the issues if you can. I grew up and I just learned to stop looking for an apology and for things to be perfect; it's just not worth it. It can't be, because she'll never be what you're looking for. Just move past that expectation that she would ever apologize or be the mother that I would want her to be. I just let it go, because I knew it would just poison the relationship that we do have now.

Today, her mom is still a disappointment, and her dad is aloof. But Cheryl isn't going to end her relationships with her parents, ever, because having a parent—specifically a mom—is most important. Cheryl says, "I just let it go. I just don't think about it." You "only get one" mother, and you must make it work with the one you have. This relationship is essential and cannot be filled by anyone else; due to the compulsory nature of kinship, the parent-child tie is irreplaceable regardless of the quality of the relationship.

Cheryl's story reveals how the socioculturally endorsed belief that the parent-adult child tie cannot be replaced is deployed as an explanation for persisting in this relationship. Many of the LGBTQ adults we talked to feel, like Cheryl, that they *have* to stay in relationships with parents because that's simply what family means—all in line with compulsory kinship.

"Your Obligations Are Much More Important Than Your Love"

The relationship between Bruce, a sixty-year-old white gay cis man, and his stepmom, Carrie, a seventy-one-year-old straight white cis woman, offers another view of the rationale of uniqueness. Bruce's parents divorced when he was nine or ten. He lived with his mom after his father, a physicist, moved away and married his stepmom, Carrie. For most of his childhood, Bruce's biological mom was addicted to pain medication and was unable to provide in any meaningful way for Bruce. This led to periods of not having enough food to eat and, as Bruce describes it, a "basic poverty situation." Bruce knew he was gay from a young age, but he didn't tell anyone because in his mind "to be gay in a situation like that is basically a death warrant."

When Bruce turned sixteen and his mother's addiction escalated, he moved in with his father and Carrie—a more "middle- to upper-middle-class" family—and their three sons; his mom passed away shortly after Bruce moved out of her home. Carrie was, according to Bruce, "a very different kind of lady" than his biological mother, while Carrie describes Bruce as "more dramatic than the other boys." In her interview with us, she echoes Bruce's description of the financial differences that existed between these homes, noting that she was "shocked" at the "shack" Bruce was living in with his biomom:

> When we were dating, I said to Paul, "Well, you know, what if your kids would come and live with you?" "Oh, my kids will never come, [my ex-wife] would never let me have the boys." I think he felt because of the money. I mean, she wanted the check, you know, the child support I think. . . . I'm certain that she loved her children in a certain way. But I really think she was impaired.

The move to his dad and stepmom's home stabilized Bruce for a time, but this stability came to an end when Bruce turned eighteen and was asked to move out on his own. He graduated from high school and went to college, but "nobody in my family had gone to college before so everybody was just like 'You crazy?'" Still, he earned a bachelor's degree and moved to Florida, where he found a supportive and loving gay community. But even this joyful period was short-lived due to the spread of HIV/AIDS. Bruce explains, "That was devastating for me. Everybody that meant anything to me in my entire life died." He too contracted HIV. "When I found out what that was, and I said, 'Ah, I'm just gonna go off myself, and go out quietly.'" But instead he made his way back to the Midwest to reconnect with his dad and Carrie.

Even though Bruce had a college degree and work experience, he spent several years living paycheck to paycheck, sometimes in severe debt; his stepmother described him as "not a very good money manager." But Bruce explains this his situation isn't a result of his inability to save but rather the result of an economic system that discriminates against disabled people. He hit a rough spot due to severe health problems that forced him to quit his job. Unable to get financial assistance through disability payments, even though he had the appropriate approval, Bruce spent a period of almost a year wherein he lived without income. During this time, Bruce experienced serious financial hardship that "brought me to my financial knees. I mean I had no money, and when I tried to reach out to my brothers, they helped a little bit, but then they got angry at me for asking for too much."

Unable to pay for rent or food, he ended up living on the street. His biomom had passed away years before, and Bruce's dad had died a couple years prior, so he couldn't ask either of them for help. Instead, his stepmother "came through in a big way." Bruce explains, "I was out in the street—I think I was staying over at [a fast food restaurant] in the rain. And I literally didn't know what I was gonna do." It was his stepmom who stepped in to help. He explains, "I came to my stepmother," who had "come into all this money from dad's death." Bruce thinks she gave him money because she felt guilty. "If it weren't for my father," he notes, "she wouldn't have had nothing. But he set her up" before he died. Bruce was grateful and surprised at her help, noting that before this "nobody's given me shit."

This gift lifted Bruce out of homelessness. While his parents had failed to provide the safety net he needed throughout his life, he frames this one gift as a sign he should stay in a relationship with what's left of his family—notably his stepmom. When asked to tell us more about how he feels about his stepmom today, Bruce says he wishes they were closer, saying the lack of closeness is "having a devastating effect on me right now" because he doesn't have many other intimates due to the HIV/AIDS epidemic. He is grateful he has *some* relationship with his stepmom. "So my family—I can't claim all of it is so bad." He goes on to explain that despite the pain, he stays connected. "It's about obligations and fulfilling your obligations, and there isn't a whole lot of love, you know love and affection and all that stuff is sorely needed, but your obligations are much more important than . . . your love. That's the way it works." The expectation that the pair fulfill the basic role of a stepchild and a stepparent, however limited, is keeping this tie intact.

Bruce firmly rejects the rationale of love and closeness as a way to explain his persistent family bonds. And his parents and brothers certainly haven't gotten more accepting over time to allow for any illusion of growth. Instead, he recognizes that what makes a family is obligations embedded in the roles of parent and child—or stepchild and stepparent—rather than love. Despite the years of strain, he is still their child, a role that is full of meaning and obligation. A sense of duty binds parents and children, cementing the uniqueness of the parent-adult child tie.

"I'll Always Be Her Kid"

Erica is a thirty-two-year-old queer Latina lesbian cis woman who provides our final illustration of the rationale of uniqueness. Erica grew up in East LA with her "very, very small family" of just her and her mom, Miranda, a seventy-two-year-old white "sexually fluid" cisgender woman who moved to the United States just before Erica was born. Erica's dad had significant drug problems that have left him virtually out of her life, although Miranda still gives him money on occasion. Miranda explains that Erica's father "decided not to get close to Erica because he didn't want to be the kind of father his father was. So he was pretty distant, even though he loved her, he adored her, but he was very distant."

Erica and her mom have "always been really close," with her mom treating her as a little adult from the time she was young. "We were all that each other had," she explains, saying that, as immigrants, "we don't have other family." This relationship has continued in strength even after Erica moved across the country for school, with Miranda saying, "We're really good friends. I think she trusts, I hope she trusts me. I think we're just really, really close now."

Erica's story is a little different than others we've presented because her mom is also queer. "My mother came out when I was about ten. I really had no pressure at all to be any kind of person," says Erica. Miranda concurs, saying, "I think she has her sexuality fluid. So her coming out was nothing. It was like no big deal."

Instead, their conflict regards Miranda's lover (and Erica's stepdad). Erica's stepdad and his kid moved in unexpectedly when Erica was a teen, "and nobody said anything to me about it." This greatly upset Erica because, as she explains, "I was an only child, and I was used to being alone." Erica and her stepdad's relationship has never recovered from this rocky start. “It’s always been very difficult,” Erica says, because has traditionally tried to insert himself between me and my mother and has caused problems that way. Actually, he and I didn’t speak for about three years, and then finally, I was just like, ‘This is ridiculous. I’m not doing this anymore.’ We started speaking, and now, I try to include him.”

At one point, Miranda temporarily stopped this romantic relationship in order to prioritize Erica. To explain this decision, Miranda draws on notions of family uniqueness:

> He wanted us to have a relationship. And I said, “No, my daughter needs me.” Not only does my daughter need me, but I need to repair that relationship with her. First and foremost. Not for me, but for her, because she doesn’t have anybody. We have a very, very, very small family. We’re immigrants and we really have nobody. What we have is each other. And I said . . . I cannot abandon her, no matter what. And I will not, under any circumstances. And if that means being alone for the rest of my life, then that’s what I’ll be. Not that I wanted to live with her, but I have to show her that she matters. I have to show her that, that she has unconditional positive regard like that. So that was really the driving force for me, was just showing her that I was there for her.

Like Miranda, Erica also draws on notions of uniqueness to explain their persistent bond despite this conflict: “There was a lot of upset at the time, but now I know that that’s who my mother is, because ultimately, I’ll always be her kid. She doesn’t have to work to keep me. She knows she’ll never lose me. And that’s fine. I told her that I’m not going to stand for somebody coming between us again. What can I say? She doesn’t have anybody else if she doesn’t have me.”

No matter what, the tension between Erica and Miranda and the others in this theme is overcome by the rationale of parent-child *uniqueness*. The bond between mother and child is privileged above all else, and both parties expect this relationship to continue in the face of any conflict. This belief isn’t *inherently* true. Miranda could certainly choose her partner over her daughter, and Erica doesn't always have to think about herself as Miranda's kid. But this is how they are framing their relationship, all in accordance with the rationale of uniqueness that upholds compulsory kinship.

Conclusion: There's No Place Like Home

The people whose stories are told in this chapter firmly believe once a child always a child, and once a parent always a parent. Even if children feel their parents are inadequate or even terrible, keeping the identity and labels of parent or child is paramount. The parent-child tie is unique, the people we talked to insist, and no other social relationship could take its place at the core of the family. Even if parents are bad parents, they're the only ones you have.

In arguing that no one can replace their parents—and that they will always be their parents' child—our interviewees highlight our final rationale of compulsory kinship. Adults do not have to stay in relationships with parents who fail to live up to the standards of care, but so often they do. While low-quality marriages, friendships, and jobs often end, powerful sociocultural messages tell us that even very low-quality parent-child ties are too unique to be broken. Parents are your family, plain and simple.

Black and Latinx people in our study deploy the frame of uniqueness in clear and consistent ways highlighted in this chapter, although white people relied on this rationale too. Black and Latinx families have been typified as disrupted and "broken," in need of fixing, by outdated and racist social commentators.[4] What we see in this chapter, however, is the strength of Black and Latinx parent-adult child ties through the dedication to staying together forever. Due to both living in a racist broader culture and being a marginalized group in the United States, Black and Latinx people may have fewer opportunities to experience social belonging more broadly outside of their kinship ties.[5] Even as Black and Latinx people have long built a broader family network of kin that include not only parents but also friends, neighbors, aunts, and grandmas, parents—especially mothers—remain *highly valued* social ties.[6] In Black families, in part because of the unjust disproportionate rate of mass incarceration of Black men, Black mothers are often seen as a pillar of family life.[7] In Latinx families, the value of *familismo* creates deep, unbreakable bonds between parents and kids—again especially mothers—perhaps in part because familial solidarity is necessary for survival and self-identity.[8] We suspect, and past work suggests, that there may be unique cultural factors that elicit a particularly strong belief in the "irreplaceable" parent-child tie in families of color despite—or perhaps because of—the racist social and economic forces that continue to restrict and shape the family lives of people of color in the US today.[9]

While relationships between parents and children don't *have* to be primary in the conceptualization of the family, they *are* without doubt central to family identity in the United States today. The parent-adult child tie is influenced by a culture of compulsory kinship that keeps people bound to parents even when these relationships are not great. We as individuals are embedded in this system that sees the parent-child tie as central and unique to family life in the absence of other possibilities. There are other ways to organize family life, but the powerful forces of compulsory kinship make it nearly impossible to leave parents behind.

We return to the question of alternatives to the primacy of parents in the conclusion of this book. But next, in part II, we move to address *how* people actually stay in not-so-great relationships with parents.

PART II

How LGBTQ Adults Adhere to Compulsory Kinship

In part I, we presented three socioculturally sanctioned rationales of compulsory kinship—love and closeness, growth, and uniqueness—to explain *why* LGBTQ adults stay in relationships with parents. In part II, we focus on *how* LGBTQ people adhere to compulsory kinship and stay in relationships with parents. Our answer is relatively simple: people do *family work*—and more specifically *conflict work*—to maintain these relationships.[1] We think conflict work is key in the everyday operation of compulsory kinship.

"Family work" is a sociological concept that includes many subsidiaries, but broadly defined, it refers to the effort made to promote family functioning.[2] At first, family work was used to show the disproportionate labor cishet women do in the home to care for the household and children. Notably, this work has historically been devalued and unpaid, making cishet women's labor a site of gender inequality. Drawing on Hochschild's concept of emotional labor,[3] "emotion work" was identified as a new type of the family work, theorized as the efforts to either hide or change one's emotional state to convey a curated sense of self through the face or body.[4] Like housework and childcare, emotion work is disproportionally done by cisgender women married to cisgender men, again with detrimental effects on gender equality within the family.

The concept of "kin work" was added to the family work umbrella to highlight the efforts done to maintain multihousehold extended family connections through letters, visits, gatherings, and gifts.[5] Di Leonardo coined the term "kin work" when studying Italian American families in California.[6] Women in these families worked to sustain relationships within and between familial households, with kin relationships often deteriorating without women's influence. But since its conception, kin work has been studied most seriously within Black families. Stack and Burton show how Black families do kin work to "regenerate families, maintain lifetime continuities, sustain intergenerational responsibilities, and reinforce shared values."[7] For example, Black mothers do intensive kin work to include other family members in their children's lives—putting in particular effort to keep the fathers of their children, as well as grandparents, aunts, and uncles, involved in child-rearing. Kevin Roy and Megan Reid show how Black fathers do kin work, too, to create a safe space in their neighborhood where they can interact with their children, keeping fathers integrated within their broader family units.[8]

The broad concept of family work and the subconcepts of kin work and emotion work cover much of the intentional labor done to keep the family unit functioning and intact, with some negative consequences for those who disproportionately do this labor. What is missing, however, is consideration of the specific work of maintaining family relationships when there is serious conflict between one or more family members. Thus, we argue that family work should be expanded to include "conflict work," which we define as *the effort done to manage severe conflict in a way that ensures family functioning*. Much like other forms of family work, conflict work privileges the family being intact over an individual's needs.[9] In the case of our study, LGBTQ people privilege the persistence of their parent-child tie over the need of full acceptance and a healthy family dynamic.

In chapters 5 through 9, we show how LGBTQ adults do intensive conflict work to stay in the family, adhering to compulsory kinship even when the conflict is due to parental rejection of their LGBTQ identity.[10] Much as kin work can be more readily seen in Black families because these families are marginalized by the interlocking systems of oppression of colonialization, the prison industrial complex, and white supremacy, we argue that conflict work is more visible in our sample of LGBTQ adults and their parents due to the forces of homophobia, heteronormativity, and transphobia that are dominant in the United States today. And, given that the systems of racial-ethnic, gender, and sexual oppression overlap, in the next chapters we pay particular attention to how conflict work is racialized, gendered, and shaped by homo-, queer-, bi-, and trans-phobia together.

First, we visit *the kin closet* to show how white and Asian LGBTQ adults actively use the closet to manage anti-LGBTQ discrimination and stay in their families. Next, those LGBTQ adults who exit the closet often become a "teacher" at *gender and sexuality school.* LGBTQ adults—especially those who are gender expansive—make great efforts to educate their parents as a way to maintain, and hopefully improve, their conflictual parent-child relationships. If education doesn't work, some white, Black, and Latinx LGBTQ folks use conflict work to move *under the rug* to stay in the family—either by their own volition or by being pushed under the rug by their parents. However, white cis gay and lesbian people sometimes leave the rug and do the conflict work of *becoming normal.* This occurs when folks access the "normative" statuses of spouse, partner, and parent to appeal to parents in ways not readily available to LGBTQ people of color or white gender-expansive people in our sample. In the final chapter, we show one last strategy of conflict work: being *out of the family*, wherein people cut parents out for a time to keep the relationship intact for the long term. This form of conflict work was done by people of all race-ethnicity and gender identities and almost always resulted in an eventual return to the family.

These strategies for keeping families together aren't static. LGBTQ people move in and out of different conflict work strategies to stay connected with their parents, all the while trying to maintain their own sense of integrity and well-being. The LGBTQ people we talked to shifted across different strategies to stay in the family. In the end, tremendous effort and multiple forms of conflict work are needed to keep families in line with compulsory kinship.

5

The Kin Closet

Corey's parents divorced when he was eight, after which he spent most of his time with his mother. "My relationship with my mother is much better than mine with my father," Corey explains, as his dad wasn't there for him throughout his life. The fatherly absence left Corey feeling "upset, bitter, cheated," the effects of which continue to shape the pair's relationship today.

The now twenty-three-year-old white cis man told his mom he's gay a couple of years ago. The conversation went well enough and didn't cause any major issues, although his mom is still a little tense when discussing his sexual identity. But, coming out to his dad "just never happened." Corey recalls, "I was never at a point in our relationship where I was like, that kind of needs to happen." He trails off, thinking about whether he ever will tell his dad he is gay. He comes up empty-handed, saying, "whether or not that happens . . ." and shrugs the question away. When pressed about what would happen if he did come out to his dad, Corey answers, "I don't know." Corey *thinks* his dad won't care, saying, "I haven't just randomly been like, 'Yeah, dad. I'm gay.' . . . Whether or not that conversation happens soon, it might. I don't know." But Corey's next thought reveals he has a deeper worry of rejection. "Really, the only two people in my life that don't know are my father and grandfather," he says, noting that both are "extremely religiously conservative." So, Corey doesn't tell his dad, protecting his intact albeit distanced relationship, while also reassuring himself that his dad "won't care."

When we started this project, we expected that most people would be out of the closet with their families—especially because the closet has been framed as something we are "beyond" both as a society and in adulthood.[1] But for many people like Corey, the closet is absolutely vital to maintaining parent-child relationships when parents exhibit homophobia, biphobia, and transphobia. The fear of the unknown, even if accompanied by hope that a parent would be accepting as Corey suggests, often led people to keep their sexuality or gender identity secret.

In this chapter, we tell the stories of those who have decided that the best way to stay in their parent-child relationship is to remain in the closet—at least at the time of our interview. To show how the kin closet works today, we first take a brief look at how the closet has operated for LGBTQ people historically.

The Closet

In the mid-twentieth century, the closet was the default residence for LGBTQ people. During the Lavender Scare of the 1940s and 1950s, the US federal government fired anyone they suspected of being a "homosexual."[2] Later, during the 1990s, the "Don't Ask, Don't Tell" policy meant that gay and lesbian people serving in the military were forced to stay in the closet or leave the military ranks. During this same era, it was illegal to engage in consensual same-sex sexual acts in some US states, and queer bars were routinely raided with their patrons being jailed and publicly shamed in newspapers. Meanwhile, being trans was heavily stigmatized and considered among the worst social ills.[3] Same-sex sex was criminal, being LGBTQ was immoral, being trans was a mental illness, and the closet was the only place to hide.

In response to this repressive climate, a new social movement arose, marked as beginning most famously with the Stonewall Inn riots in Greenwich Village, New York City. The anti-police riots led by queer people of color at Stonewall, many of whom were drag queens, ushered in the new gay liberation movement of the 1970s.[4] This movement dovetailed with HIV/AIDS activism in the early 1980s, enacted in response to the federal government's culpability in the death of thousands of queer people.

The effectiveness of this movement in gaining legal rights for cis gays and lesbians is significant and essential to recognize.[5] In 2003, the case of *Lawrence v. Texas* led to the repeal of antisodomy laws in the United States, and in 2011, "Don't Ask, Don't Tell" was repealed by President Obama, allowing gay and lesbian people to openly serve in the military.[6] This was followed by the legalization and broadening public support of same-sex marriage—first in Massachusetts in 2004 and more than ten years later federally in 2015.[7] The gay rights legal era culminated in 2020 when the US Supreme Court ruled that LGBTQ people are protected legally from employment discrimination under the Civil Rights Act of 1964.[8]

These legal shifts were accompanied by significant social changes. Young adults today disclose their LGBTQ status more often and earlier in the life course than any previous generation,[9] with the closet morphing from an oppressive mandatory residence to something one could *actually come out of*. "Coming out" became understood as a rite of passage in the developmental process of becoming a "healthy" LGBTQ-identified person, especially among white middle class people, where staying in the closet went from being a life sentence to a relic of adolescence.[10] In 2004, Scott Seidman famously wrote that we are "beyond the closet" in the United States, although the very notion of the closet as something we can be beyond has been critiqued as a white cis gay notion.[11]

Despite Seidman's claims, there is plenty of evidence to suggest that the closet is still in residence—at least for some. LGBTQ people today face intensive homophobia and transphobia across all regions of the country.[12] And, the closet is alive and well in the lives of the people we talked with—in particular, white people.[13]

Instead of facing potential vitriol and risk being kicked out of or leaving the family, the people in this chapter use the closet to manage *perceived* or *potential* conflict with parents. If children suspect that their parents won't be able to address their own intolerance, and if children don't want to or can't afford to leave the family, then the closet is a safe harbor. The people we talked to discussed three types of closets. First, some discuss dad's closet, where LGBTQ adults don't tell their dads about their identities. Second, some gender expansive people discuss the trans-itional closet, where trans people keep all or part of their trans identity in the closet. Third, there is a bisexual closet, where bi people avoid disclosure unless absolutely necessary.

Dad's Closet

Dads and moms parent differently, not because of inherent or biological gender or sex differences but because of our adherence to and performance of strict gender norms in the family. As a result, moms are consistently told of a kid's LGBTQ status first, while dads are often the last to know.[14] And this is for good reason. The gendered expectations of what it means to be a dad—which are explicitly focused on a lack of emotional availability or open communication and being more prone to aggression or violence—mean that many LGBTQ adults feel especially unsafe or uncomfortable sharing their identities with their fathers.[15] Dads can exert spectacular pressure on their sons to act masculine and their daughters to act feminine, and overall dads more strictly police what is considered acceptable gender for their children.[16] Fathers often see their LGBTQ children's gender and sexuality as a failure of their parenting.[17]

Why tell dad if his response will be bad? In the context of presumed homophobia and transphobia, and the straight cisgender imperatives of masculinity and femininity, it makes sense to keep dad out of the loop—especially when compulsory kinship means this tie must remain intact. If dad responds poorly, and *you can't or don't want to leave this tie* due to compulsory kinship, why risk it? Dad's closet allows people to remain in relationships with their fathers, but also protect that which is personal and precious.

Like Corey, described earlier in this chapter, Marco stayed officially in the closet due to the limits of his dad's masculinity. Marco, a fifty-three-year-old gay white cis man, grew up with his mom, dad, and six siblings. He remembers figuring out his sexuality early on, stating, "I mean everyone knew that [I] was gay when, if I guess it was puberty of, you know, twelve, thirteen, fourteen, whatever it was." He told his mom, who responded well enough, but his dad passed away without explicitly knowing about Marco being gay. Marco simultaneously defends and judges himself for his lack of disclosure. He asks why *he* should come out when his siblings didn't have to come out as heterosexual? They just lived their lives, they got married, and had children. They didn't have to say they were straight, and so, he says, "I didn't think I had to say I was gay."

But he pauses to question his motives about why he never told his dad. "To be honest," he says, "I did not want to have that conversation with dad." He worries that this news would have hurt his dad; it would have been too much. "It was my dad," he explains. "I think he'd been through enough, to be very honest with you," referring to the illness that eventually killed him. Marco projects what he thinks his dad would have thought, which is, "Good lord, now I've raised a gay son! What the hell's going on?" He continues:

> I think he would be hurt, and back then, gay was not good. Gay was you were kind of a freak, you were weak, and you didn't have much of a life ahead of you because you didn't have family. You wouldn't have children. You would be ostracized socially and you fled to New York or San Francisco. I mean, you certainly couldn't go around in [Midwestern city], so I think he would be really upset initially.

Marco didn't want his dad to have to deal with his own, or society's, homophobia. Or maybe he didn't want to come face-to-face with his dad's reaction. But he worries this rationale is "a cop-out," ultimately explaining he wasn't willing to chance damaging his relationship with his dad. In the end, Marco is comfortable with his decision to protect his relationship with his father by staying in the closet.

Pam has a similar story we want to share. Pam, a twenty-year-old white bisexual cisgender woman, grew up in a household with her mom, dad, and younger sister. Pam "low-key" came out to her sister first, and then about a year later told her mom, who she thinks "already knew." Pam hasn't told her dad out of fear of his reaction, even as she downplays the possibility of rejection. "It's not something I imagine he cares about one way or the other," she explains. "I feel like he'd be just as happy for me to just never date anyone. Just, shh, go find like a nice, nice academic tower to seclude yourself in, but . . . I don't think he cares."

But the very fact that Pam has not discussed her sexual identity with her father suggests that she is *not* sure of his response, either because it's true that he does not care "one way or the other" or because it would be uncomfortable or stressful for the relationship. Pam's use of the closet with her dad is informed by her father's deeply held conservatism, which Pam expresses by saying, "The Venn diagram of things we agree on has become two, like, deeply far away circles . . . there are just some conversations I don't want to have with him." Pam says she has "reached the acceptance stage" on this topic. "It's like this is just how you are, and I can try to make a dent in it, or I can remove myself. I just have to accept that 'cause you're my dad, and that's how you are." So far, Pam has used the closet to avoid a possible negative reaction. Because he will always be her dad (i.e., the rationale of uniqueness from part I), Pam tries to protect their relationship and adhere to compulsory kinship by not coming out.

Trans-itional Outness

Although public support for same-sex marriage and gay and lesbian people in general skyrocketed in the first two decades of the twenty-first century, there was simultaneously continued significant marginalization of those gender and sexual identities that are considered less mainstream.[18] In 2017, twenty-seven states attempted to institute so-called bathroom bills meant to restrict trans people from using public restrooms.[19] In 2020–2021, nearly two dozen state governments put forward legislation to regulate both trans people's participation in sports and trans youth's access to gender transition and affirmation medicine.[20] And exactly four years after the shooting at the Pulse nightclub in Orlando, Florida, where forty-nine mostly LGBTQ people of color lost their lives and fifty-three others were seriously injured—nearly all of whom were Hispanic or Latinx—the Trump administration removed protections against health care discrimination for trans individuals. Trump also banned transgender individuals from serving in the military, removed guidance for schools to treat transgender individuals in line with their gender identity, and allowed emergency shelters to discriminate against transgender and gender-expansive individuals. [21]

In the context of this legal and social discrimination and violence, relationships between parents and their trans kids can be incredibly tense. As a result, many trans people in our study used what we call the strategy of trans-itional outness to stay in relationships with parents—at least for a time. Commonplace notions of coming out are, as Orne explains, "predicated on Erikson's linear model of identity development, [wherein] early theories conceptualized coming out as one stage among a larger series of steps," always moving toward an end point of outness.[22] But for many trans people, coming out is a continual, nonlinear, context-specific set of moments that are never over and always redone.[23] Since gender can shift throughout our lives, coming out or disclosing one's identities often requires multiple passes, either to clarify one's own identity or to note a change in identity. Thus, trans outness is in transition.[24] Some trans people we talked to stepped out of the closet as gay, lesbian, or bisexual with no mention of their gender to avoid parental rejection.[25] Others disclosed their trans identity but purposefully held back the meaning of this identity to minimize conflict. We discuss both approaches here.

Out as Gay, Not as Trans

We introduced Jackie, a fifty-four-year-old white trans woman whose sexuality is "evolving," in chapter 2.[26] There, Jackie explained she stays tied to her parents because she believes that *deep down* they love her, regardless of the pain they have caused her. Despite this belief in overriding love, she made the decision to tell her parents that she is HIV-positive and gay but not trans. As she puts it, "I didn't come completely clean. I left little spots." After a bit of a pause, she laughs and says, "Actually, a big blotch. It was hard enough to explain gay to them, much less trans." Today, only her younger sister knows she's trans, and she is totally unsupportive of Jackie's transition.

Jackie hasn't come out as trans to her parents because she wants to get along with them. In this way, the trans closet allows her to preserve her relationships. In talking about using the closet to stay in touch with her dad, Jackie says, "I try not to get in his wheelhouse, and I don't let him in mine." Her wheelhouse includes her gender identity. When asked how her mom would react if she learned of Jackie being trans, she says, "I don't want to say my mom would disown me." But her long pause after this statement implies that deep down Jackie is afraid her mother will do so. In addition to a fear of being disowned, Jackie is afraid her mom will ask, "What did I do wrong?" To which Jackie would reply, "'Well, you did a lot wrong, but this has nothing to do with that.' I guess I could tell her that, 'You did a lot wrong, but this is not any. . . . One of the things you did wrong is not treating me like a girl, but you didn't know.' I guess I never liked to trouble people."

Jackie's plan to not cause trouble relies on the timing of her parents' death. "We still have this generation that, in my opinion, [we need to] let them die. Why try and shove things down their throat, that they just can't get. I'm not saying we shouldn't live our lives," she insists, "but they'll never understand and why get pissed at them if they don't? They have no concept. They're who they are." Still, today, Jackie is on estrogen and has started to physically look the way she feels inside, encouraged by a group of polyamorous and gender-expansive friends she made after she got divorced. She is deeply anxious "about being femme" with her parents, but "now it's getting hard [to hide my gender]. I actually have to grow my hair another two inches before I can get this into a ponytail.

There's nothing I can do to make this look like boy's hair. Bangs are down to here now, so they go back to here. I'd have to wear a very, very strong sports bra." She goes on to say that she doesn't plan to ever come out, if she can help it. "I think I'm trying to outlast my mom and dad," but she's unsure if this will happen.

Jackie likes the protection the trans closet provides her. "I don't want to do the whole trans thing with them," she insists. Jackie's closet is protective, a key conflict work strategy that in her mind keeps her in the family. Given the significant pain that comes with parents willfully misgendering you or rejecting you in other ways,[27] staying in the closet is an adaptive approach to maintaining her parent-adult child ties.

Out as Trans, but Still Have Secrets

There's another way trans people use the closet to stay in the family: being "out" as trans but allowing the meaning of a trans identity to be ambiguous. Grady, a twenty-three-year-old white bisexual trans woman, exemplifies this type of conflict work.[28] Figuring out her gender identity was quite difficult for Grady. She recalls, "Growing up, you know there is something different about you. But I didn't even know transgender was a thing until I was like twenty because I live in such a small town." As Grady figured it out, she came out to her mom in stages: as bisexual when she was a teen and then as trans a year or so ago. But Grady explains that now her mom, who Grady lives with, only *sort of understands* her trans status—and this is purposeful on Grady's part. Grady has slowed the process of explaining, keeping parts of herself in the closet to avoid harming their relationship.

When Grady came out as trans a year ago, her mom "kind of denied it." Grady explains, "I don't think she really cared the first time, and she was really not great about it. She told me I could do whatever I wanted, and she couldn't affect that, but she didn't really like it that much." Now, after some long and hard talks, her mom "has gotten a lot better about things. We go shopping and spend more time together and stuff." But,

Grady explains, while her mom may be coming around to accepting her being trans, she doesn't really understand the *meaning* of trans, noting, "she even told me she didn't understand it."

Grady does not have the energy to do the intensive gender education to help her mother understand her (see chapter 6 for more on gender education). This includes Grady's name change, which she hasn't told her mom about. She's afraid to tell her "because basically I'm going to be taking something that I've had for twenty-three years, that she gave me, and just shitting on it. It terrifies me how she's going to take it." Grady even found some greeting cards she's considered sending her mom to try to explain her gender further. "On the front it says, 'Surprise, I'm a girl.' I thought about writing it in there, but I don't know. The fact that I'm changing everything she knew is what scares me, for her reaction." Grady keeps not only the name change in the closet but also the real effects of hormone replacement therapy (HRT). While her mom knows she's on HRT, Grady explains, "I don't think she knows the extent of things." She is afraid of her mom's reaction when the full effects come to light.

Grady is working hard to protect her relationship with her mom—and herself—by disclosing only as much as she thinks their relationship can take. Although her mom understood and adapted to Grady's bisexuality, she does not understand all aspects of Grady's trans identity. This, Grady thinks, is because being trans is just not well understood by the cis community. "In the public eye and in the media and stuff it's definitely a lot newer. Because when it comes to the rest of the LGB community, they've been fighting for decades, and it's been in the public eye, and it's been out there." Noting how trans people have been excluded from the broader rights movements, Grady says, "Whereas trans people, we're just starting our fight, and people are just figuring this out, worldwide."

While her mom is the primary parent in Grady's life, her dad is also around. Grady is not very close with her dad and is certainly not out to him. Still, she explains, "We're on good terms and it's not like we're estranged or anything. I just don't talk to him a lot or see him a lot. I just kind of live my own life." Yet, akin to the "dad's closet" theme presented earlier in the chapter, Grady hasn't disclosed her bisexual *or* trans identity to her dad for fear of his reaction. As she sees physical changes in herself, like her breasts developing due to HRT, she knows she will need to share this information, but she's afraid of how he'll respond. She has written a letter to help explain to her dad what her gender means, which says:

> Hey, Dad, I'm writing this because I have something to tell you, and I don't want to say it face-to-face. You were wondering about all the stuff I'm doing at my doctor's appointments. Well, I'm trans, and what that means is that who I am doesn't correspond with my body, since my brain works separate from my born sex. My brain is female. It's not uncommon and it's not a problem, and there are other people like me. There's nothing wrong with it, and I'm changing it and becoming who I am. This is happening. You can support it and that would be great, but if you don't I will understand. But it's happening anyways and I would love for you to be there.

Grady highlights the ongoing process of (not) coming out, showing in her narrative how she has (not) come out at different times to differing degrees based on the relationship. In doing so, Grady shows how the closet operates in service of compulsory kinship, keeping adult children in the family by limiting full information flow.

The Bisexual Closet

Just as trans people have unique experiences with the closet due to societal and interpersonal transphobia, bisexual people have a unique closet because of the particular social stigma and stereotypes about bisexuality; bisexual people often feel that when they partner with someone of a different gender, they are read as straight; when bisexual people partner with someone of the same or a more closely aligned gender, they are read as queer or gay/lesbian. In both cases, bisexuality as an identity is not fully visible. While invisibility is sometimes seen as a source of stigma and strain in other contexts, when it comes to the parent-child relationships of Whitney and Bonnie, bi invisibility is helpful for staying in the family.

Whitney, a twenty-two-year-old white bisexual cis woman, grew up with a sister, mom, and dad who divorced when Whitney was ten. The divorce was a "big relief" because she never liked her dad, who was "very strict, very rigid" and emotionally and verbally abusive; her mom kicked him out after a physical altercation between the spouses. While this created a more emotionally stable environment, Whitney lived in poverty and used food pantries and government assistance to survive without her dad's financial support.

Whitney and her mom are still tied together in financial and emotional ways, while she and her dad are quite distant. This has implications for her not coming out to either parent as bisexual. Reminiscent of chapter 2, which details the deployment of the rationale of love and closeness to explain persistent ties, Whitney says, "Like, I'm close to my mom, but it's never been a relationship where like you tell her a lot of things. She definitely has more of kind of like an older style of parenting." When asked how Whitney thinks her mom would respond to learning of her being bi, Whitney says, "I'm not too sure about [her]. I think she would come around. I did try to tell her once, and I just kind of brought up the whole subject itself with her. And she kept going on with like Bible verses, so I just dropped it. I think she would come around, but I think at first there would be like a huge conflict."

Her dad's potential reaction is particularly worrisome because, as she explains, "My dad said when I was younger, if I dated someone of another race or was gay, that he would disown me. So I'm guessing that's probably still the case." Her dad's deeply held racism and homophobia are connected, with both white supremacy and homophobia used to control his daughter's sexual behaviors. The legitimate fear of rejection and conflict, both historical and current, personal and societal, is the reason Whitney is hesitant to come out to her parents. Whitney wants to maintain these relationships in line with compulsory kinship. Her parents' racism and biphobia mean she has to use the closet to do so.

Still, the fact that she's not out to her parents weighs heavily on her mind. She is a strong proponent of LGBTQ rights, and even led a gay-straight alliance in college for three years. In that space, she got some pushback for not being out. "There were a lot of people that would comment on that when we talked about coming out, that I'm the one running things, but I haven't even told my own parents," she explains. However, she reflects on this decision: "I mean, it was just kind of a decision that I made. I was like—maybe it's for the best not to bring it up." Whitney will likely stay in the closet with her parents for the foreseeable future. "I just kind of decided that it was better just to kind of keep those views separate for the most part," she says. Again, revealing the contradiction of the ideal of closeness and love from chapter 2, she concludes by saying, "I know this sounds strange for being close to them too." Using the closet to protect her relationship with her parents, Whitney creates and maintains less tension and stress in her own life while maintaining their relationship, using bi-invisibility to protect these ties.

Like Whitney, Emelia uses the closet to stay in relationships with her parents. A twenty-year-old bisexual cis woman who was born in Southeast Asia, Emelia grew up living in the United States with her mom, dad, brother, and grandmother and recently moved to the Midwest for college. Emelia doesn't share a lot with her parents, including her suicide attempt or her sexual identity, explaining, "I don't know, if I can't even tell them that I tried to kill myself, I wouldn't be able to tell them that I'm like, bi, right?" But she has provided "hints" to her parents about her being bisexual, akin to what McLean calls "testing the water."[29] "I told them I went to Pride, which was like a pre–coming out. So I haven't like completely come out to them yet, I hope to." She explains, "They asked me what I was doing that day, and I just said I'm going to the Pride weekend event parade. And they said, okay or have fun or something like that, so I don't think they really got what Pride was." Later, when Emelia posted a picture of herself at Pride holding a bisexual flag on social media, she was surprised when they Facebook "liked" it. "I don't think they know what [the flag] meant," she laughs, "you know how old people are. But I was holding a bisexual flag."

Emelia is teetering on coming out of the closet but can't seem to find the "right" way to do so. She doesn't think her parents understand what the bisexual flag symbolizes and assumes that the deep denial she knows many parents have about their own kid's sexuality means they won't make coming out easy on her. But how does she think they'll react when she does come out? Emelia says, "I don't think they would react." This doesn't mean they would be accepting; she literally means they *would not react*: "They would just pretend that I didn't say anything, and it was a phase." She thinks this is related to her parents' racial-ethnic background, explaining, "It's a very Asian thing. I'm very certain about that. . . . They would definitely talk about it but they probably would just come out with the conclusion that I was joking."

For Emelia, the closet works to maintain her family but also allows her to continue to develop her own sense of identity. When asked if she would want to ever tell them, she says, "Oh, if I'm interested in someone of the [same] gender then I feel like I, yeah, I would tell them." Emelia will come out as bisexual, but not until she needs to—that is, until it becomes a visible and legible part of her life (via a relationship), a tactic described by McLean as "selective disclosure."[30] But for now, she likes her conflict- and judgment-free relationship with her parents and uses the closet to maintain that. Why come out if it would only cause strain with her parents? She is in the closet, but the closet at least keeps her in the family home.[31]

Conclusion: The Closet as Conflict Work

In this chapter, we show three types of closets that operate to keep the family bonded—dad's closet, the trans-itional closet, and the bisexual closet. LGBTQ adults in our study maneuver within and around the closet to keep peace in the family, especially when dads are involved. In choosing who to be out to and how out to be, the people we talked to stay in line with compulsory kinship and remain in the family. Interviewees prioritize their parent-child ties in the face of parental homo/bi/transphobia, maintaining these relationships the best way they know how right now: by using the closet.

Instead of the closet being (only) a repressive site that one should get out of, we found the closet was often seen as a *necessity* to keep peace in the family—a *central tool LGBTQ adults use to stay in their families.* In the midst of the continued stigma of queerness in the United States, and the Midwest more specifically, the closet privileges the family over the individual. And while being in the closet may indeed be oppressive, it can also be the only recourse to managing these ties in a homophobic—and, in the case of this chapter, especially transphobic and biphobic—family system.

In our study the closet is used primarily by our white and Asian interviewees. In a chapter titled "Beyond the Closet as Raceless Paradigm," Marlin Ross notes that white queer scholars and theories "are beset by what I call 'claustrophilia,' a fixation on the closet function as the grounding principle for sexual experience, knowledge, and politics."[32] Following Ross's critique, it is possible that our Black, Latinx, and Indigenous interviewees also see the closet as a white artifact they have no relationship to and thus do not use.[33] For example, Mignon Moore explores how the "coming out" framework does not adequately capture the experiences of Black gay people, that instead the concept of "coming into the life" discursively explains Black people's experiences.[34] We also note that some of our Black and Latinx interviewees discuss a variation of the closet, *being under the rug*, a phenomenon akin to what Black scholars have suggested is more apt for Black LGBTQ people, discussed in chapter 7.

Before we get to the rug, however, we want to present the second approach LGBTQ people use to stay in relationships with their parents: gender and sexuality education.

6

Gender and Sexuality School

We introduced Natalie, a forty-six-year-old straight, bisexual, gay, lesbian, queer, pansexual Black trans GQ/GNC woman, in chapter 4.[1] There, Natalie deploys the rationale of uniqueness to explain her continued bond with her transphobic mom. Here, we want to discuss the conflict work that Natalie does to actually stay in the relationship: specifically, education work.

Natalie came out as trans about six years prior to our interview, right around the time she got divorced from her then wife. Throughout most of her adulthood, including her marriage to a cisgender women, Natalie knew "there was something deeper inside, you know? I just didn't know what that was." This is because throughout most of her life transgender was "more of a clinical term," and instead she identified as a "cross-dresser for years." Now, she explains, "transgender has become a hot-topic word, or a buzzword," and this has allowed her to step into this identity more confidently.

Today, Natalie does conflict work to try to get her mom to understand her gender identity through education—with some success. Natalie's mom often uses her deadname and makes transphobic comments; Natalie blames this on her mom's "instinct" as a member of the Black Baptist church. "I mean we can have that conversation from time to time and I can tell her how I feel," she adds, "but it has to be very casual." She tries to further explain what "casual" means when she is educating her mom. She gives an example of this kind of approach:

> There was this article in *Time* magazine. Laverne Cox was on the cover. . . . And, I sent [my mother] the magazine. I put sticky notes on the page, and I said, "You need to read this." The article basically just talked about trans

people. Talked about the struggles of trans people. It talked about suicide. It talked about the suicide rate amongst trans people. . . . Several months later she came back, and she's like, "You know what? I love you. I'm proud of you. You could have easily decided to just kill yourself, but instead you decided that you were gonna fight, and I stand behind you." That was uplifting to me. I think that she understood. I think we had a subsequent conversation. She was like, "Well, how do you deal with people who want to challenge you on religion and the whole nine yards?" I was just like, "I deal with them on a case by case basis, and we can talk about it because I personally feel like God loves everybody, and I don't think that God hates people who are gay, or hates people who are transgender."

Natalie is working to change her mom's transphobic beliefs to improve their relationship and ultimately to allow her to stay in the family. Her mom still deadnames her, but Natalie explains this is because she's old and has a lot on her plate. Sometimes, though, Natalie will try to gently remind her mom of her name and pronouns, noting, "It can be frustrating, because it's like, I paid money to have my name changed. I wanted my name changed, and yet you're calling me by this old name." Still, Natalie stays in the family—and within the bounds of compulsory kinship—through educational conflict work.

The Gender and Sexuality Factory of the Family

The family is a gender and sexuality "factory" wherein one of parents' chief jobs is to produce "properly" gendered and sexual adults.[2] From bedroom decoration to clothes to the pronouns and adjectives used to describe children (e.g., pretty, strong), to heterosexualizing children and romanticizing childhood different-gender friendship dynamics (e.g., a crush, a heartbreaker, a flirt), so much of parenting in the United States is rooted in creating heterosexual, cisgender people.

In the current era, parents have authority over children's gendered and sexual selves with power over not only what children *do* but also who children *are*.[3] Parents model the acceptable qualities they wish to see in their children, teaching children what it means to be heterosexual and cisgender men and women.[4] This begins before a child is even born, with gender reveal parties mistaking chromosomal or anatomical characteristics with gender; after the child is born, parents expect sex assigned at birth to correspond to gender.[5] (For example, the logic goes: a penis = a male = a boy; no penis = a female = a girl.)[6] Thus, parenting decisions from conception on are rooted in sex and gender dichotomies and the conflation of one biological characteristic with sex, and sex with gender,[7] with most parents giving children gendered toys and clothes.[8] In turn, parents normalize and expect heterosexuality from the moment sex and gender are "decided" by doctors and parents. This heterogendering occurs throughout childhood when parents refer to different-gender "crushes" instead of friendships, when parents and teachers frame heterosexual procreation as a goal of adulthood, and with the rampant acceptance of homophobic and transphobic norms.[9] Further, any hint of gender nonconformity—especially among sons—is quashed for fear it is a sign of homosexuality given the assumed link between gender and sexuality.[10]

In this context, a kid being LGBTQ is definitely not celebrated, with parents often linking their children's gender and sexuality "normativity" to their own success as parents.[11] Parents continue to try to make their children heterosexual and cisgender into adulthood. But in this chapter, we show that adult children are able to fight back against parents' power. Here, LGBTQ adults begin to combat essentialist anti-LGBTQ beliefs, much like the young trans kids in Meadow's *Trans Kids* (2018), by using the conflict work strategy of education to combat the years of anti-LGBTQ bias.

Through the stories of Natalie, Melissa, Lorraine, Aly, and Jake, this chapter shows how gender-expansive people, in particular, carve a safer place in the family by teaching parents about their identities. Most LGBTQ people who were out in our sample tried to educate their parents about their identities at some point, but gender-expansive people seem especially dedicated to educational work as their primary approach. While there has been widespread acceptance of LGB people in the United States today, gender-expansive, especially trans, people remain a key site of sex and gender panic.[12] The belief that there are only two binary sexes and corresponding genders that remain consistent across the life course (and that these genders are complementary via heterosexuality) is so deeply ingrained in US culture that many find any other organization of sex, gender, and sexuality inconceivable. While efforts for gay and lesbian rights—most famously the successful bid for same-sex marriage—have effectively mainstreamed white gay cis men and lesbian women, many of our gender-expansive interviewees are excluded from acceptance, understanding, and affirmation.

US society stigmatizes, pathologizes, regulates, and ostracizes gender-expansive people. When children move out of the binary gender system, or away from their sex assigned at birth, it is parents who most protest, often using what stef shuster calls "discursive aggression" to try to hold their children accountable to their sex and gender assigned at birth.[13] Discursive aggression "regulates trans people in everyday social settings and produces for them the feeling that they are not received in the ways they wish to be known, that they are made invisible, and that their self-authorship in naming and claiming a gender identity is questioned." As a result, gender-expansive people have to do especially intensive gender and sexuality education with their parents. In addition, the gender-expansive people we talked to also had to do serious education work around their sexualities, not just their genders, as their sexualities don't often fit into the neat, more mainstream boxes of gay and lesbian. As such, we focus on the stories of gender-expansive people's educational work—in terms of both sexuality and gender education—in this chapter.

C+ Sexuality Ed Student Parents

Melissa, feels lucky she grew up in a relatively stable home with her mom, dad, and older brother. Now twenty-three years old, she says her family is "not great" at communication, calling her mom "passive-aggressive" and "micro-managey." But her parent-child relationships have been, in her words, "fine."

Melissa, a white genderqueer, gender-nonconforming, queer and pansexual person, is more independent than her brother, who still lives with their parents as an adult because he struggles with anxiety, social interactions, and holding down a stable job. Melissa struggles with anxiety, too, explaining, "I get panic attacks, and then I also have just generalized anxiety a lot of the times too, like throughout the day, it's just kind of there." Melissa's mom, Shannon, a fifty-four-year-old white straight cisgender woman, blames this on Melissa being a high achiever: "When she was younger, she's always pushed herself very hard to be the best she can. Sometimes that causes a little anxiousness."

Melissa got bullied a lot in school, and while kids teased her about being gay due to her gender nonconformity, she was "definitely not going to admit to any of this." But in college, she finally admitted to herself and her mom that she was "not straight," using this vague terminology in part because she just didn't yet have the language to explain her sexuality. She told her mom over dinner at a restaurant, "I need to tell you something, I am not straight." Her mom responded nonchalantly, "Yeah, I know. Do you want an appetizer?" Melissa laughs when she tells this story but also finds it disconcerting. Did her mom really understand? Does it matter?

Shannon describes this moment in a similar way, "I guess I didn't see it as a bad thing or a good thing. It was just a thing? Coming out wasn't a big deal. I mean, people are what they are." But Shannon also knows that Melissa was insecure about her reaction. "I don't know. Maybe she wanted us to be more excited or something?" Shannon summarizes her lackluster response, one she has given to Melissa several times: "So it is what it is." Melissa hates this reply. "I kind of wished she asked some more questions, because she's very much just like, 'Yeah, I don't really care. You can do whatever.' But it was very big to me at the time."

Melissa didn't trust her mom fully, believing this response was indicative of rejection. Instead, Melissa decided to do education work to bring her mom toward the level of acceptance, understanding, and support she expected. The first time Melissa tried to do education work was after hearing Shannon refer to her as gay. Melissa replied, "'Actually, I'm not gay. Let's talk about this now.' Because I was like, 'I did a really bad job coming out if I just said I'm not straight.'" Melissa is trying hard to explain herself again to her mom, telling her, "'Let's talk about language. Different words you can use. This was actually more how I identify. I identify more as like pansexual, or like fluid.'" To this educational effort, Melissa says her mom's response was "Okay, cool." This felt seriously dismissive to Melissa.

After her lackluster coming-out experience with her mom and her repeatedly unsuccessful attempts to get her mom to talk about her identity, Melissa was worried about talking about her sexuality with her dad. Like those in chapter 5, Melissa didn't tell her dad for a year or two, noting, "I guess we never had really deep conversations, and I don't call him to update him on my life." Melissa felt awkward and afraid about what he would think given the barriers to open communication between many kids and their dads, as well as the norms of masculinity that structure the father-child tie. But now she's starting to question those assumptions. "I started to realize that I really don't talk to my dad about anything happening in my life, so I've been trying to do that a little bit more," she explains. Recently, he asked her, "Hey, I've been thinking about this. And I want to be able to . . . I just don't know how to talk to people on Facebook about these things." Melissa realizes the problem is that she's "never talked to him about how I identify and other language within the LGBT community." He doesn't have the tools, including what "queer means." Melissa was excited to explain these meanings to him. In our interview, she relates another conversation detailing the education work she does about her sexuality with her dad:

MELISSA'S DAD: So you're not a lesbian, but what word do you use for your relationships?

MELISSA: What do you mean, my relationships? Like what? What does that mean?

DAD: What's your relationship called?

MELISSA: Do you mean, how do I identify?

DAD: Maybe?

MELISSA: Okay. So I don't identify as a lesbian, because my two previous partners have been trans men. That doesn't make sense.

DAD: Oh, I see that now, because they're not women.

MELISSA: Yes, they are men.

DAD: So what do you call the relationship?

MELISSA: I identify as pansexual, and then this is how my previous partners have identified.

DAD: Oh, okay.

Despite Melissa's reluctance to try to educate her dad on the differences between lesbian (attracted to/has relationships with women) and pansexual (a person attracted to/has relationships with any gender), this conversation began a series of education work sessions that she feels went really well. For Melissa, these conversations "don't feel intrusive," and this reaction is much better than her mom's apathy. Her dad is seriously trying.

Melissa does ongoing sexuality education with both her parents. While her mom remains reluctant to be a sexuality student, her dad is accepting and encouraging of this education, making her feel much closer to him. The family still has a ways to go—especially since she has yet to tell them about her gender-nonconforming identity—but her educating them on her sexuality has been a key way Melissa stays in her family.

Failing Out of Gender School

The gender-expansive people we interviewed do intensive, often exhausting, work to educate their parents about their gender identity.

Yet, not surprisingly, many parents fail gender class.[14] This is the case for Aly and hir parents.

Aly grew up with hir parents in rural Appalachia and then moved to a nearby city for college to put some distance between hir and hir parents. Aly realized ze was trans/genderqueer and queer sexually when ze took a gender studies class.[15] The white, now twenty-three-year-old saw a poster in class depicting a trans/enby person. "I said, 'Oh, that's it. I've got it.' And I decided not to tell anyone at the time, because I wasn't sure how that would be received, and I wasn't too sure about it myself."

After college, Aly was forced to move back home for economic help and told hir parents about hir identity. Aly's parents reacted very poorly and kicked hir out of their home, leading Aly to move in with hir grandmother after graduating. Aly cut off hir parents for two years because of their rejection of both Aly's queer status and hir subsequent queer marriage. Aly explains:

> As my father puts it, [there was a] failure to embrace. . . . Basically, they were not being supportive of anything about me. They were not supporting my life choices, and my mother was constantly threatening to cut off my phone and other things like that if I did not do what she wanted. And so I got annoyed about it, and decided, "Okay. If you don't stop threatening me and generally criticizing me and saying that I'm doing everything wrong, we're not going to speak." And they did not stop, so we didn't speak for two years. . . . Honestly, that time period was very stressful . . . but that [not talking to my parents] was the most relaxing thing about it. Talking to them in general is very stressful.

We discuss estrangement further in chapter 9, but here Aly explains that cutting hir parents off gave hir new power. "Now it's: 'I refuse to participate in any drama so do not bother me about any of these things or I will not answer your phone calls for a year.'" These boundaries give hir a new ability to be hirself and to work toward creating the kind of relationships ze wants with them.

The high level of strain around Aly's gender and sexual identity was echoed by hir mother, Margaret, a fifty-five-year-old straight white cisgender woman. Prior to the estrangement between Aly and Margaret, Aly relied on hir parents for some financial help. When Aly changed hir name to reflect hir gender identity, effectively coming out, a significant conflict began that had financial implications. Margaret talks about this conflict; we retain her original quote but note Margaret uses she/her/hers pronouns for Aly, which Aly does not use:

> [Aly] just called us and said, "Well, I've changed my whole name. You have to call me Aly now." And when she [*sic*] did that, I will be honest with you, I feel like she divorced the whole family at that moment. . . . I don't make very much money and she doesn't work and I think she's got, you know, mental problems. So, to help her be able to live in [city], me and my husband were sending her $100 every payday. Now that might not seem like much to you, but his check is only $700. . . . So I had been doing that the whole time that she's up there. Every two weeks we would send her $100. And when she did that, I thought that's it. I'm done. So I quit sending her money. Because I thought she divorced me. I thought "You want to divorce me, and not even talk to me about this or ask me how I feel about it?" It was just like she just ripped my heart right out when she did that. I just felt like she divorced the whole family, and I was just done.

Aly changing hir name impacted how Margaret felt about Aly as a member of the family, resulting in Margaret removing much-needed financial support. When asked why Margaret started talking to hir parents again, finances again played a part for Aly. "I talk to them now because, well, I can't afford my own phone bill, and my health insurance is with my father," ze explains. "It's not a very good relationship, but I do try to have like casual social contact as well." Both finances and relationship uniqueness are rationales for keeping this bond intact.

For Margaret, the relationship is tense at best. Margaret thinks Aly just "wants to fight with me all the time." And yet, Aly's relationship with hir mom remains intact despite being significantly "hostile." It's clear from Aly's perspective that what hir mom calls fighting, ze calls education. Ze does intensive conflict work to educate hir parents about hir trans and genderqueer identity, reporting few successes and many failures.

One failure that stuck with Aly is when Margaret told hir: "I have picked to be everything she hates, and can't she have a normal daughter, and all of that kind of stuff . . . and that in particular really bothered me, because she said that I picked to be everything she hates." Aly explains why this is so wrong: "So for one thing, apparently being queer and trans is a choice, and she actively hates queer and trans people, and she thinks I am doing this to spite her, I guess?" Ze laughs, saying, "Which I feel this is a lot to do to spite someone's parents. Like good lord, I don't have that kind of energy. But she emphasized that she was hoping it was going to be a phase, and that I couldn't be mad at her for using the wrong name or anything like that, because she named me, and that's the most important." Aly's mom draws on the status of "mother" and name-giver to assert power and shame over Aly's decisions.

But in response, Aly explains that hir mom consistently plays the victim about Aly's identity and "acts like I'm being mean to her by telling her to use different words and names." Aly reflects on how hir mom reacted to hir name change:

> I made her feel like I divorced the family by changing my name, and she makes everything about her feelings, which I don't think she's not allowed to have them. By all means, have whatever feelings you do, it's just she makes them the only relevant part of the situation a lot, and so she will consistently be like, "Well, you can't be mad at me. I'm trying." And, "This is so hard on me, don't you understand? Like you're my baby, I've called you this for twenty years, of course, I can't just change your name." And

> she makes a lot of excuses and generally presents it as though I am being cruel by saying to use different words.

Aly focuses on a particularly hard educational moment with hir mom about hir pronouns and name. "She thinks that she should be able to use my birth name, and she/her pronouns if she is talking about the past, even in front of me, because back then I was a girl, I guess, according to her understanding." Aly is trying to give hir mom credit for her faulty logic, but in the end ze is frustrated. "I've tried to explain multiple times that's not true. But it's more work. She ends up saying it's too much work, you can't expect this of people." Aly sees the work as necessary to get them to stop deadnaming or misgendering hir:

> Last time I saw [my parents], my father called me the wrong name. And I was like, "Hey. That's not me. Try again." And then he was like, "Oh, that's right." And it really bugs me when people won't correct themselves after I say something. I know it's kind of persnickety, but I want people to be like, "Oh, sorry. Aly." That's the one. Because saying it will reinforce that that is [my name]. And then it will help them in the future to remember not to do that.

In one effort to educate, Aly tried to teach hir parents about ze/hir pronouns. In response, Margaret told Aly, "That sounds like a made-up language." Aly finally concluded that "it wasn't worth it to continue fighting. So it was like, 'Okay. Gender-neutral pronouns then. They. You know how to use 'they.' That'll work.'" Unfortunately, even "they" doesn't really work. Aly tells the story of a recent encounter, saying, "I didn't say anything until after she had finished her sentence, and stopped talking, and then was like, 'Hey, by the way, still 'they.' Good try. But still 'they.'" In response, Aly's mom got angry and stopped the conversation.

While Aly sees some progress due to hir education work, tensions and transphobia persist. Margaret herself explains:

> She'll [incorrectly referencing Aly] just jump all over you if you accidentally say "her" . . . she gets very angry. I just handle her with gloves. . . . I let they call me, um, because they just want to fight with me all the time so it's just better if I just don't, if I, um, just let they call me. Now not that I don't want to see that person, 'cause I do, but I don't want to fight. And I'm tired of getting attacked. And, you know, this threw me into a deep depression, when this all first came out . . . about a year ago, I decided that I deserve to be happy, and so if just staying by myself and letting . . . they contact me, then that's how I'm going to do it. Because I don't deserve to be attacked, or beat up, when I was a good mother. Not all because of a pronoun. I don't deserve this. . . . So, you know, I'm not going to leave myself open for being attacked.

Margaret continues to struggle with pronouns, even in our interview. "I'm going to quit worrying about this pronoun when it's just me and you," she says to Emma, who interviewed her. "It's just throwing my speech pattern off and it's just making nervous. So we just won't tell her [*sic*] that—but I just want to talk normal." Aly's gender identity is still, unfortunately, a deep source of conflict in their parent-child relationship. But Aly continues to use the strategy of education work to address these issues to maintain this tie—even as Aly's mother does not acquiesce to this approach.

Gender and Sex Ed: A-for-Effort Moms, Failing Dads

Given that the parent-child tie is gendered, with parents of different genders having distinctive expectations and guidelines for children of different genders, approaches to education work look quite different even in the same family. This is the case for Lorraine and Jake, who we introduce here.

Lorraine is a twenty-one-year-old white genderqueer/gender-nonconforming and gender-questioning gay person who has lived with her twin brother and her mom ever since her parents divorced when she was six. Lorraine's mom got full custody after the divorce, and the pair are close; Lorraine hardly saw her dad during her formative years, in part because he spent months away from the family as an active marine.

Despite their closeness, things haven't always been smooth sailing for Lorraine and her mom, who is "really conservative" and has always "voted Republican"—shorthand for being homo- and transphobic. Lorraine's mom grew up in a small town in the Midwest as "a white woman, poor . . . just not knowing much about homosexuality." Lorraine's mom's only understanding of being gay came from the homophobic media of the 1980s. "So," Lorraine explains, "from my earliest memories talking about gay people isn't particularly positive."

This conservative backdrop made Lorraine worried about coming out to her mom. Lorraine's mom didn't disown her like Lorraine feared, but instead she expressed worry about how much harder Lorraine's life would be "because people are going to treat you poorly." Despite good intentions, Lorraine's mom "didn't understand that some things she said were hurtful," like asking homophobic questions and repeating antigay rhetoric. But Lorraine knew her mom loved her (i.e., the rationale of love) and was willing to try to become an ally (i.e., the rationale of growth). "It was a learning process for both of us," with both Lorraine and her mom working through things together, keeping the relationship intact.

After Lorraine came out, her mom went to meetings of Parents, Families, and Friends of Lesbians and Gays (PFLAG) at Lorraine's request. From there her mom started to "kind of figure what words she shouldn't say or should say. She subscribed to the LGBT community." This was huge for Lorraine because her mom "made it a big deal to understand and kind of became more and more progressive." These changes are not without their difficulties, as there is still some need for more education work. "As much as she has changed, and she's definitely always changing, progressing, there are some things that she still doesn't understand," Lorraine explains. "She feels like sometimes I'm too harsh about her, too harsh to her. And I probably am. It's just kind of frustrating, and I kind of snap quicker with her than I would with someone who doesn't unconditionally love me." But this "snapping" takes a toll on Lorraine. "And then I feel bad about it, and she feels bad about saying the wrong thing, and then we apologize to each other." This encounter happens time and time again.

The pair's struggles have recently been more apparent because Lorraine is finally moving beyond sexuality education towards educating her mom about her gender. Notably, Lorraine's gender identity is still shifting, and she is coming to understand herself as genderqueer, gender nonconforming, and gender questioning. In fact, Lorraine has already faced pushback on her gender expression. "I think our main source of conflict is my appearance," Lorraine explains of her new exploration into gender nonconformity. "Definitely unfortunately a product of our culture's opinions of appearance and how women should look and act and everything." Lorraine further explains that this conflict means she won't be coming out as genderqueer/GNC anytime soon:

> I have been feeling out the idea of a lack of gender, and trying to explain the concept of gender-neutral pronouns to my mom, who is, like I said, very, very accepting, but also . . . she doesn't understand the concept of singular "they." Her brain, she just can't do it. Which is fine, it's not malicious or anything. She just physically can't get her brain to consistently use them. So, because of that, I probably won't ever end up using singular "they" pronouns.

For now, Lorraine is okay with not using "they/them" pronouns (with her mom, or otherwise) or her mom fully understanding her gender identity. She thinks she'll keep trying to educate her, though, as she has been receptive so far. Despite some struggles, Lorraine and her mom continue to teach and learn and are committed to improving their relationship. Both are willing to do the educational conflict work to stay together.

Lorraine's mom's growth due to deep education work—even if uneven around gender—contrasts sharply with her dad's unwillingness to learn. Lorraine hardly talks to her dad, but he does periodically drop into her life. She has had to come out multiple times to him, and each time he states her sexuality is "wrong." She says, "I had to keep reminding him [of my identity], and then he would just forget again. Just kind of actively trying to tune me out." But this hasn't deterred Lorraine. She explains, "But, now, I've just made an effort on the few times a year I see him that I say, 'Oh, yeah, I'm doing this thing for the LGBT community' or 'Yeah, I went to Pride a few weeks ago' or stuff about cute girls at school." She does this over and over again to try to help him understand that her sexuality isn't a phase and it isn't wrong.

Despite this work, Lorraine's dad is still unaccepting. "He's said a lot of things that are very homophobic, and obviously his politics very much support people that are homophobic . . . he's kind of a dick." She keeps trying, though, and says now her dad "will like my posts on Facebook about Pride, so it's kind of this weird, not hypocrisy, but it doesn't match up." This contradictory behavior extends to her brother, who has recently started wearing dresses—behavior her dad "cannot wrap his head around." If her dad continues to be unteachable, Lorraine will consider cutting the tie completely.

This story of Lorraine's dad's resistance to learning and mom's growth is similar for Jake, a twenty-nine-year-old white queer trans man who has engaged in significant gender education with his parents. Jake, who grew up living with his brother, mom, and dad, describes a tense family bond and an emotionally and verbally abusive father. "To be honest," he says, "I don't know why they're still married. I don't know why they got married in the first place. I wish my mom had just booked it and got out of there because my dad is not exactly the ideal parent." He adds, "If I could trade my dad for even a fictional character, I would." His relationship with his brother is not much better; Jake describes it as "hateful," in part because he believes his brother is his dad's favorite. Every Christmas and birthday Jake would make a list of what he wanted, but "my brother's getting the shit I wanted, and meanwhile I'm getting the girly shit because I'm a girl." What really bothered him was his parents saying, "Girls don't play video games."

Jake came to understand his sexuality first, coming out to his mom as gay in 2009, with little fanfare. But he explains, "I never felt comfortable being referred to as a girl or referring to myself as a girl. It just didn't fit, and no matter what I did, I could not get rid of that feeling." Eventually Jake started talking to friends and found a forum on the internet in 1999 for people who felt like him. But it wasn't until he turned twenty-seven that he felt like he really had a grip on who he was. He went through "weeks and weeks and weeks of just sweating myself insane over this, and finally I broached the subject with my mom" when his brother and his dad weren't home.

While the conversation was uncomfortable for Jake, his mom was quite willing to be educated about his gender. When he told his mom, "There was a lot of really awkward parts of the discussion, but we talked about it, and then finally mom was like, 'Okay. I don't get it, but okay.'" He explains, "When there's a transgender issue my mom doesn't quite get it because she's not trans. She's cis, and so she doesn't really understand why something gets to me." But Jake works hard to give his mom the benefit of the doubt and try to teach her. "She'll say something offhand, and it's not meant to be malicious, it's not meant to be othering, it just is and I have to explain it."

Gender education isn't always easy for Jake to do. Due to Jake's anxiety and mental health issues, he must be careful with his energy because this education work is draining. And if he doesn't have the energy, or his mom "doesn't have the head space to pay attention," there is a "disconnect" between the pair. Still, Jake does the work to stay in the family, especially with his mother because she has tried to understand and learn. "My mom slips up, but that's my mom. My mom's also older," Jake explains. "She's unlearning everything that she was taught."

Jake stays bonded to his mom because she's open to education work. But in contrast, he says, "My dad? Nope. No chance in hell." Jake's dad "had a fucking fit" when he found out about Jake's gender identity from Jake's mom. "He flipped his shit and it was like a solid two weeks of him not saying anything to me, glaring at me, getting up and storming out the door." Jake clearly remembers what his dad said when he found out, "something about 'no daughter of his is one of those tranny freaks' and shit like that, and I was just like, 'Okay, except I'm not your daughter, bitch,' and in the course of the two, three weeks he didn't talk to me, I would just open my mouth and he would just scream, but I'm like, 'Go fuck yourself.'"

After his father's abusive reaction, Jake still tried to educate him, but his father continued to fail gender school. Jake explains, "He has refused every step of the way to call me Jake, to call me he/his/him, to call me his son. It's always that name that I don't like, that I've never liked. She/her/hers. My daughter." His dad even promised that once Jake got his legal name changed and physically transitioned he would use Jake's name. But this agreement was fabricated. "He still hasn't. I've been on testosterone for a year and a half. My name was legally changed in May 2016. My ID says Jake, and my dad refuses."

Jake tried to help his dad understand his gender through education work, but it's clear the effort was wasted. Now, Jake barely talks to his dad, and Jake's brother and mother have stepped in to take some of the work off Jake's shoulders. As Jake explains, "My mom's been up his butt about it. My brother's been up his butt about it." This was a welcome relief, especially the support from his brother, who told his dad "don't talk to me" due to his transphobia. Through all this, Jake stays in relationship with his dad, but only tangentially through his relationships with his mother and brother. However, if Jake's dad does not start to become more supportive, showing some level of growth, Jake will consider ending their relationship.

Conclusion: Gender and Sex Ed as Conflict Work

LGBTQ adults do extensive conflict work to deprogram parents of their essentialist, transphobic, cisnormative, and homo/bi/queerphobic beliefs. Some parents respond well to education, even if they don't fully understand their LGBTQ kid. Others who won't try to learn run the risk of eventual estrangement.

While most people in our sample used education conflict work at some point in their lives, gender-expansive people are the real experts on the subject. Gender-expansive children confront parents' taken-for-granted, deeply rooted biological essentialism about sex and gender, retracting parents' fundamental assumptions about who their child really is. Because non-cisgender identities are not yet widely understood, because being gender expansive often involves changes in names and pronouns, and because gender is such a visible feature of our everyday interactions, gender-expansive adults have to do constant work to have their gender affirmed and understood.[16] As the stories we told in this chapter show, gender-expansive people who have less common sexual identities—such as pansexual or queer—also need to do work to explain and educate parents on their sexuality. Education, then, is a primary form of conflict work gender-expansive people do to stay in their family and maintain these kinship ties.[17]

We note that people in all of the racial-ethnic groups captured in our study used sex and gender education, but because some people didn't elaborate on this particular theme in their interviews, we chose to highlight those interviewees who talked at length about these processes—most of them being white gender-expansive people. Indeed, for some people we talked to, including many LGBTQ people of color, educational efforts were cut quite short due to negative responses to the efforts; in turn, LGBTQ people of color in particular quickly moved on to either the conflict work of the rug (shown next, in chapter 7) or briefly leaving the family (chapter 9). Next, we discuss going "under the rug" as another conflict work strategy in the toolbox of LGBTQ adults.[18]

7

Out of the Closet, Under the Rug

Bruce, the white gay cisgender man in his sixties who was introduced in chapter 4, never actually said the words "I'm gay" to anyone in his family. While he assumes they know, "they don't talk about that. They don't wanna know about that. It's not in their repertoire of what they can deal with." Instead, Bruce's family "can only deal with me if I stay on a level that they're willing to live in. That level is, 'this is my world, this kind of stuff doesn't exist. If it does exist, I don't see it,' you know what I mean?" Bruce is willing to hide who he is from his family of origin because being out of the family is not an option. All parties involved take part in positioning Bruce under the rug, with his family conveying, "'Yes, it's okay with me, but don't talk to me about it, don't ask me questions, don't ask me how I feel about it, don't bring it up.' So they really *aren't* okay with it. And they're not going to be okay with it, because you can make them very uncomfortable and embarrassed." Bruce uses his position under the rug—with his sexuality known but never discussed—to play by *their* rules and stay in the family.

As discussed in chapter 4, Bruce's stepmom, Carrie, is his only living parent. She, too, feigns ignorance. "You know," Bruce says, "it's just, 'don't bring it to the table and we don't have to discuss it.'" Carrie, a seventy-one-year-old white straight cisgender woman, did participate in our study but never mentioned Bruce's sexuality—and in order to maintain confidentiality neither did Rin, who interviewed her.[1] Carrie deflected a general question about Bruce's dating history, to which she replied, "But he was, um, you know, physically, he was just small. And that's tough. For boys that's tough." Later, she mentioned, "He had two close friends. . . . I thought they were just close friends. One boy I liked, the other boy I didn't like." When retelling a time in Bruce's history she explained of his social group, "You know, AIDS was an issue among that group of people at that time. And, um, I felt really disgusted with him." Still, she explains that Bruce "didn't discuss it with us. You know, he didn't bring it up." She purposefully skirts around Bruce's sexuality throughout the interview, even as it is entirely apparent.

Carrie is grateful Bruce never tried to tell her about his sexuality, and she certainly hasn't asked. "It didn't do any good to talk about the negative things because there wasn't anything you could do about it . . . what good does that do?" Carries says. Both Bruce and Carrie acknowledge that they avoid any conversations around Bruce's sexuality—a "negative thing" in Carrie's eyes—because they know talking about this topic might sever their relationship. Having this shared pact to not discuss Bruce's sexuality is how the relationship persists.

In and Out and Back In Again

When closet and education work strategies fail, sweeping an LGBTQ identity under the rug can serve as a safe way to remain in the anti-LGBTQ family house while tacitly being known as LGBTQ. Some LGBTQ adults prefer it this way, while others like Bruce were forced to not discuss their identity by their parents. Either way, living under the rug is a key conflict work strategy used to stay in the family.

The use of the rug aligns with contemporary critiques of the very concept of the closet we first introduced in chapter 5. Disclosure isn't a onetime process; instead, being "out" is something people do (or don't do) over and over again—sometimes having to come out multiple times to the same person.[2] Being under the rug is akin to Carlos Decena's concept of "tacit knowledge"—meaning something that is unspoken but known.[3] In Decena's work, Dominican immigrant gay and bisexual men inhabit a space of being both "in" and "out" to others, where there may be tacit knowledge of a gender or sexual identity but it is not always referenced in interactions. In a similar vein, Katie Acosta's work on Latina women in same-sex relationships shows how these women *deploy invisibility*—a version of what we call the rug or Decena calls tacit knowledge—to minimize family stress and maintain family of origin relationships. As Acosta writes, "If making their same-sex partnerships invisible helped ease familial stress, these women often found ways to do so because, by keeping their families of origin content, they were ridding themselves of potential stress and frustration."[4]

In the following stories, we add to this line of research to show another example of how LGBTQ people push themselves—or get pushed by parents—under the rug in service of compulsory kinship.

Lonely Under the Rug

Leslie's parents divorced when she was eight, with her mom doing "everything in her power to keep my dad out of the picture." Her mom was quite effective, although Leslie and her younger sister would have visitations with their dad once a month. As a result, Leslie's relationship with her mom was deeply impactful in her life for better or worse, while her relationship with her dad was quite limited, even in adulthood.

The now thirty-year-old white lesbian GQ/GNC/trans woman realized she was gender expansive when she was twelve, a moment she describes as making everything "click." But her mom both ignored and chastised this revelation. For Leslie, realizing she was trans "but then not being able to do anything about it" was, in a word, miserable. She retreated into herself for the next six years—a time she describes as a period of constant darkness—going "full goth" by wearing a black trench coat and boots constantly. With her goth sensibility and stellar academics—taking college classes in high school and graduating early—her fellow "tractor-driving" rural high school classmates picked on her relentlessly. Leslie's mom noticed her depression and suicidal ideation and made her go to therapy, but the therapist was a Christian counselor who would not allow Leslie to talk about her gender. Leslie's trans status became a "topic that wasn't allowed to be discussed." Period.

Leslie found herself under the rug. "I had the trans part figured out early on," she says, but after being denied by her mom, "everything was on hiatus. I wasn't out. I actually didn't tell any of [my friends] until right about the time I graduated high school. Right before I graduated, I came out to my best friend," who responded with affirmation. In fact, Leslie graduated early so she could come out. On the night of graduation she left her mom's house, moving to a nearby city with some friends who knew she was trans. She was thrilled at her new life. "I was so far in the closet during middle school and high school years that I came out again post–high school and I was on my own, able to make my own decisions. I made a beeline toward transitioning ASAP."

In this newfound freedom, she once again told her mom she was trans. But, just as when she was a child, her gender revelation was again swept under the rug. Leslie's mother refused to acknowledge Leslie's identity, with Leslie explaining that her mom "has a bad habit of whenever she doesn't agree with somebody, getting upset and giving people a silent treatment." In response, Leslie would "just step away. There was no point then. She is incredibly stubborn, and so it would be a waste of any sort of effort." Leslie didn't bother telling her dad about being trans, knowing he wouldn't respond well either.

Like many young trans people, Leslie had to grow up fast and make it work financially on her own. Coming from a poor family and being rejected by her mom meant that she had nothing to fall back on when she got down on her luck. A series of traumatic events, including housing and job insecurity and a sexual assault, left Leslie again in a dark place. Seven years ago, "things just sort of fell apart financially, transition-wise, education-wise." She could no longer afford her hormone replacement therapy, she wasn't able to secure loan money to continue her college education, and her car broke down, making it impossible to get to work. It was all too much for her to cope with, and she attempted suicide—what she called "a cry for help." She remembers thinking at the time, "We'll see how things go. Either it'll be over or I'll get help. One way or the other, things will change." She woke up in the hospital, relieved.

Leslie's parents both came to the hospital to visit her, and she views this as a point of transition in their relationship. Leslie explains, "There was actually dialogue after that, which was much better than before where there was no talking, no contact for the most part. Especially with my mom." Her mom might ask her questions from time to time about her gender, and she struggles with Leslie's pronouns and name. But ultimately, "I've come to the conclusion that that's going to be the way it is with her. She turned sixty this year, she's set in her ways. She isn't going to change." Education work hasn't really been effective, so Leslie has decided to try to downplay her gender as much as possible to stay in relationship with her mom. She doesn't want to lose her again.

Her relationship with her dad was also a bit improved, even as he doesn't acknowledge her trans status at all. Her dad paid for the hospital bills and to fix her car, which was a huge relief. In fact, today he includes her in his life a bit more and does try to help her financially in other ways. "He'll ask me to come over, and they'll make me dinner, and he'll give me gas money and a few bucks for helping out and whatnot, we'll hang out. So, I mean, he makes an effort to help me out and have a relationship with me. And much more so actually than my mom." Still, despite these minor changes, she and her dad have "come to an agreement and standstill that there's certain subjects we don't talk about. Being trans is one of them. He's not okay with that."

Leslie accepts this under-the-rug status because she wants to remain in relationships with her parents. "I've come to accept how far we've gotten is remarkable compared to other people's relationship with their parents," she says. "Given the choice between the current situation and not having a relationship at all, I'd go with the 'don't talk about certain things.'" Given the specter of total rejection and estrangement, she's fine under the rug if it means she can stay in the family.

Pushed Under the Rug

Meredith, a white twenty-eight-year-old queer (sexuality) genderqueer/gender-nonconforming woman, describes her home environment as controlled, with little room for independent thinking. As a result of a codependent mother-child dynamic that clearly stunted her gender and sexuality development, Meredith has only recently had the revelation that "I'm my own person and I can be my own person." While Meredith says she loves her mom, she adds, "She gaslights me a lot. She tells me what I'm thinking and feeling." Meredith's description is quite different than the one provided by her mom, Leona, a fifty-six-year-old white straight cis woman, who characterizes Meredith as "very, very much known her own, like knows her own mind and very um, opinionated really . . . she kind of ruled the roost in one way or another. For most of her growing up." Both Meredith and Leona agree, though, that Meredith's dad is more of the distant "disciplinary" parent. These dynamics made Meredith feel powerless and helpless at home, leading her to daydream about running away frequently.

When Meredith was a teen, Leona critiqued her appearance as not feminine enough—an appearance Meredith understands now as queer but at the time didn't fully recognize. Meredith explains her mom has been "hard on me just about my appearance and I think a lot about my appearance was queer. You know, like, I didn't like the rules, I liked wearing boy's stuff. I liked wearing girl's stuff too, I liked mixing it up." Meredith was shamed about her gender not only by her mom but also at school by kids who called her a dyke, leaving little room for queer understanding, acceptance, and support. Meredith tried to come out to her mom a couple of times—once when she was sixteen and once when she was nineteen—but her mom "gaslit me and she said 'no you're not.'"

Even to this day, Leona does not acknowledge Meredith's gender or sexuality. Meredith thinks this is because her mom is projecting a dislike of her own sexuality onto Meredith:

> I think I honestly reminded my mother of herself a little bit. Also, it just only came out to me this past year that she used to date women in college. . . . So I think that little bit of me being like queer and proud and out of the closet is, it brings up weird feelings for her. Because she's watching me live a life she didn't choose. She's happy, though. I mean, like, my father's amazing, but yeah, I think like she sees her when she looks at me. So I think that also makes her probably feel a little jealous because she's a narcissist.

But Leona gives her own take on the operation of the rug. Leona agrees the rug is firmly in place but says this is Meredith's decision, not hers. While Leona says she has known about Meredith's sexuality for a long time, "It was like it became a secret." Leona continues, a bit frustrated, saying, "She was telling people that she couldn't come out to her parents. But my husband and I were both like, shaking our heads going, 'hmm, wonder, wonder why because we already know,' you know?" Notably, Leona didn't confront Meredith about this different interpretation of events, leaving the two with very different understandings of what is happening in their relationship.

After the struggles with her mom, Meredith hasn't even tried to come out to her dad. Like others described in chapter 5, "I came out to my mom and knew she'd tell him." Meredith says her dad has never mentioned it, and she remains under the rug. This is part of an overall disconnected relationship with her father, a disconnect Meredith thinks is perhaps because she wasn't as feminine and straight-seeming as her sister. "I just like never really tried to connect with him. I felt like he loved my sister more, so it was just kind of, like, she's thin, blonde, straight, did good in school, cheerleader, you know what I mean," describing what she thinks of as his ideal daughter. "So I was just like, that's fine, that's what they want, but that's not who I am."

Today, Meredith's gender and sexuality remain "unspoken about." She explains, "It's just like I've never felt accepted, so I never felt like it was that important to them." In contrast, Leona says that she is trying, but there's a lot to learn and she needs patience from Meredith—what Meredith reads as her mom pushing her sexuality under the rug. "It seems like there's more and more and more labels. All the time. You know, and why can't we just like, why can't we just have dinner?" Leona complains. Meredith and Leona have very different interpretations of Leona and her dad's reaction to Meredith's sexuality. Leona feels that she and her husband are supportive, while Meredith views her parents as shutting down her feelings and freedom. Regardless of the interpretation, the entire family is keeping Meredith under the rug.

Happy Under the Rug

Instead of getting pushed under the rug by parents like Leslie, Meredith, and Bruce, Elle, a thirty-year-old Black genderqueer or agender person who identifies as queer sexually, happily nestles under the rug. In spite of having a sister, Elle spent a lot of time alone as a kid, in part because their sister's health problems took much of their parents' attention. Even when their parents were physically there, "emotionally and nurturing-wise they weren't there. They weren't cruel or anything like that, they just weren't there."

Elle's parents divorced when Elle was an early teen, leaving Elle to live with their mom and see their father only periodically. This made things worse for Elle. "Growing up, my mother was not loving and compassionate," Elle explains. "She was very hard," and as a result Elle experienced "little traumas." When they did see their dad, "he was spaced out a lot." Together, they made Elle feel intense emotional turmoil. "Like, 'why don't they care about me?' or 'what's wrong with me?' So there was a lot of that type of trauma, and I dealt with the situation the best that I could, because of course I couldn't understand it."

Elle "low-key" came out to their mom as queer when they were sixteen; their mom's response was to draw on Christianity to chastise Elle. "It's perversion," their mom said. A few years ago, Elle told their mom again about their sexuality and also a bit about their gender. "I don't think she knew how to deal with the information, and so we never talked about this. And it's funny because she thought I had grown out of it at like twenty or twenty-one. But I'm just like—you know, I think I'm pretty gay now." Elle has very vaguely told their dad about their gender and sexuality but avoids talking to him about it. "He makes a lots of assumptions, but I say nothing," they explain. Elle laughs and takes a lighthearted approach to their parents' ignorance, in part because no other response seems helpful. In fact, Elle doubles down on their parents' lack of knowledge because it's less trouble. "Great," Elle says, "we don't need to talk about this. It was awkward when it came up. Let's not make it awkward anymore. You don't have that type of relationship. So let's move on, it's great." They further explain, "I'm trying to keep my head above water. I don't have time to like go into the nuance of my sexuality with you."

As a result, Elle's gender and sexuality have been an open secret. Elle explains that for most of their life, the family all took a "don't ask, don't tell" approach akin to "tacit compliance," allowing the maintenance of their familial relationships.[5] Elle knows that they talk behind their back, but "I can live with that," Elle says. "That's cool." But recently, Elle's parents started asking questions, especially about being genderqueer and agender. This is new to Elle, and they respond with anger. "I'm pissed I gotta explain myself!" Elle wants to be in the family but doesn't want to do the education conflict work over and over again to explain themselves—something gender-expansive people do extensively, as shown in chapter 6. Recently, Elle explains, "I feel under pressure when I'm around family because it's like, they want me to be myself, *and* they want me to be feminine. But they don't understand, I'm only being feminine for *you*. I'm not being feminine for me, and I'm not waking up in the morning trying to be feminine. Like, that's not a part of my identity at all, I don't feel feminine, I don't feel as a woman when I see myself because that's not how I identify." This is frustrating for Elle, but they just try to not ruffle feathers—including not asking their family to use their they/them pronouns.

Rather than doing education work, Elle sweeps their sexuality and especially their gender under the rug as much as possible with the aim of adhering to compulsory kinship. Elle's worried about being honest with their parents—about taking this unspoken topic out from under the rug—because of what Elle considers their parents' fragility. Being under the rug is fine for Elle because it brings "peacefulness. Because I'm great. We don't need to talk about this." Elle is perfectly fine under the rug and plans to keep it that way.

Conclusion: Under the Rug but at Least in the Family House

Like the conflict work done via the family closet or in gender and sexuality school, the rug is a tool that allows LGBTQ adults to manage parents' LGBTQ-phobia to stay in the family. Living under the rug is sometimes the only way to stay in the family while also being true to oneself. Under the rug, gender and sexuality operate as "tacit knowledge," wherein LGBTQ adults are out but also hidden. As such, the rug is a tool used within family life to preserve familial relationships in line with the expectations of compulsory kinship.[6]

Being under the rug is effective conflict work—work that is worth it in the eyes of our interviewees because they can remain bonded to their family, in line with compulsory kinship. The rug was used by people across the gender, sexuality, and racial-ethnic spectrums, but the different forms a rug can take reflect these different orientations. Consistent with past work, people of color such as Elle appear to use the rug purposefully and with comfort as a way to cope with not adhering to family and community norms—Elle doesn't see the rug as a problem and actually prefers to keep their gender and sexuality hidden. In contrast, white people we talked to, like Bruce and Meredith, were uncomfortably *forced* under the rug to maintain family solidarity, seeing this as an affront to their belonging and their true self. In a slight variation, white gender-expansive people like Leslie *prefer* the rug, but also feel some loss as they see room for no change in their parents and have little hope of an accepting relationship. All these slight variations on the use of the rug are important to delineate, as they suggest how this type of conflict work is not one-size-fits-all but a more complex tapestry of family dynamics that work to keep parents and LGBTQ adults connected.

8

Becoming Normal

Neil, a thirty-seven-year-old white gay cis man, had what he considers a pretty "normal" childhood living with his mom, dad, and brother until he moved out on his own in his late teens. While Neil enjoyed his independence in young adulthood, his life changed drastically with the death of his mother in 2011. Neil's father, Phillip, a sixty-one-year-old straight cis man and a disabled vet with what he describes as "a bad back, bad heart, bad shoulder, diabetes," experienced a subsequent decline in health. Neil saw no other option but to move back in with his dad. "After Mom passed away, just he couldn't be alone because Mom did a lot to take care of him."

Neil now takes care of the family finances, house maintenance, cooking, cleaning, and yard work for his dad. Neil occasionally needs to take leave from work, a privilege allowed under the Family Medical Leave Act (FMLA), to stay home when his dad's health is particularly bad, carrying his dad from room to room so he doesn't fall. Phillip describes Neil as "a good son" who has "always called me old baldy."

Despite this current level of connection, Neil's dad rejected Neil being gay for a long time. Like those described in the previous chapter, Neil got pushed under the rug for years. "I had tried to come out to my parents twice when I was younger, and both times the response was, 'Oh, you just haven't met the right girl.'" Their reaction was tough for Neil, who says, "You know, because when I was still in the closet, one, there's that whole just hiding everything and just not feeling you could be yourself." The third and last time Neil came out was in 2012, right after his mom died. Neil explains that he was particularly devastated because he thought God was punishing his family because he was gay. Phillip tells the same story, almost identically, in his interview, adding that when

Neil told him of his theory he agreed that Neil's logic may be true. During this conversation, Phillip gave the message loud and clear that Neil was going to hell. This response led to several subsequent "knockdown, drag-out fights" over the years. Phillip explains the cause of these fights. "I don't understand. I believe it's wrong, I was brought up in a Pentecostal church. And then I went to a Baptist church, which is—my wife's dad was a deacon of the Baptist church. You know what that's like. And . . . I just, I feel like, you know, he says he's born this way, I think it's a lifestyle myself personally." Phillip reconciles his faith and his son being gay with "a lot of praying."

But despite Phillip's homophobia, recently things between him and Neil have improved. While Phillip still isn't "100 percent 'Oh my, this is super wonderful,'" Neil insists "he's gotten a whole lot better about things." And Phillip agrees, saying, "We've gotten closer." What changed? Both Neil and Phillip explain that some of Phillip's change of heart comes from Neil's education work—akin to what we discuss in chapter 6. "We would be watching TV and things like that, and he would—just because of the era he grew up in, he didn't think about saying, 'Oh, well that's so gay,' that kind of stuff," Neil says. Neil rolled his eyes at these comments but then took the role of educator. "I would tell him how that . . . affected me, and he was like 'I didn't even think of it' and he apologized."

But alongside education work, Phillip's change of heart was due to the entrance of Neil's new partner, Terry. Phillip wished more than anything for Neil to be what he considers "normal": to reach the key milestones of marriage and parenthood. While a significant other would ideally be someone of a different gender, Neil's "honest man" partner is the next best thing. "He's seeing a guy now who I like," Phillip explains. "He introduced me to an honest man, he's been at the house a couple of times, a few times really. And I like the kid, I like him a lot."

Phillip likes Neil's partner, Terry, because he fits what Phillip thinks of as normal. "He has a job and he works and all this and that. Neil's happy, and I'm glad he's happy, I want him to be happy. And I don't want him to be alone. . . . [Neil] acts like he wants to have a home together with him . . . I am glad." Neil explains that Phillip is even coming around on gay marriage since he started dating his partner, noting, "When we were talking—like marriage equality and stuff like that—he's like, 'You know, I just want you to be happy.'" After many years of rejection from his very religious family, Neil is visibly relieved in his interview, saying, "Dad's so supportive of wanting me to have a healthy relationship with someone; [this] makes me feel a lot better."

For Phillip, his son being gay *and* alone is too abnormal, too weird. Once Neil begins living a life that looks closer to his own, with Neil having a job, a monogamous, marriage-ready relationship, and a future vision of homeownership, Neil becomes more legible to his dad. Even as Phillip still doesn't "believe" in his son being gay, he can now live with it. Plus, after the loss of his wife, Phillip feels he must preserve his relationship with his son, saying, "It's not worth losing somebody else." Family is forever as a result of compulsory kinship, and his gay son becoming "normal" is one way this forever family is possible.

The Trouble with Normal

While some LGBTQ adults may keep their romantic and sexual relationships in the closet or under the rug in order to stay in the family, or do serious education work to get parents up to speed on gender and sexuality today, others like Neil find that a visible and so-called respectable relationship can be a route to *acceptance* in their parent-child ties. For a select few people—all white cisgender gay and lesbian people—the conflict work of becoming "normal" is a way to secure a permanent place in the family. In this chapter, some white gay and lesbian cisgender people make great strides in maintaining their parent-child relationships by actively emphasizing their committed romantic relationships and their own roles as parents. For these LGBTQ adults, adhering to so-called normal statuses of marriage and parenthood allows parents to frame their kids as "just like me"—and thus acceptable.

This dynamic is a prime example of the concept of homonormativity, which is the transplanting of heteronormative values of monogamy, marriage, procreation, and the idealized middle-class white nuclear family onto gay and lesbian people.[1] Homonormativity works to reduce homophobia and increase acceptance of the type of white cisgender gay and lesbian people who are *almost* just like straight people. But, in doing so, homonormative approaches further marginalize those who do not fit within the privileged identities of cisgender and white. This is why only white cisgender people can successfully use this conflict work strategy.

Homonormativity has been a key tactic of white cisgender gay and lesbian rights groups, such as but not limited to the Human Rights Campaign (HRC), to gain legal rights for "respectable" (read: middle-class, monogamous, cis, white) lesbian and gay people.[2] The HRC, for example, used white cis gay and lesbian families in ads promoting gay rights, explicitly leaving nonwhite and non-cis people and their more progressive activist agendas outside of the "mainstream" movement. This homonormative normalization approach was extremely successful in obtaining the now overwhelming national public and legal support for gays and lesbians, at least in part *because* it marginalized non-cis people, queer people, and people of color—and their needs—from the movement.

As we have discussed throughout the book, trans people are consistently left out of the mainstream gay and lesbian civil rights movement, even as they are the most recent site of state and federal legislation against their very existence through bathroom bills, trans-exclusionary sports laws, and antitrans health care laws. As Susan Stryker explains, hetero/homonormative acts not only are done by white cisgender straight men who rule this country but also are done *within* the LGBTQ community *by* cis "gays and lesbians who [see] transgender issues as entirely distinct from their own and who resisted any sort of transgender participation in queer politics and culture." Homonormativity, then, was "aimed at securing privilege for gender normative gays and lesbians based on adherence to dominant cultural constructions of gender, and it diminished the scope of potential resistance to oppression," leaving gender-expansive people outside the realm of normal citizens.[3] This is similar to how Amy Brainer discusses "strategic normativity" in *Queer Kinship and Family Change in Taiwan*, where gay advocacy groups work to help kids "let mom and dad know you're the OK kind of gay,"[4] through an emphasis on monogamy and constraining nonnormative expressions of gender and sexuality identity to private spaces in order to appear "normal" in public spaces.

Homonormativity also draws on racist logics of colonial white supremacy as it relies on hegemonic white Western values to determine what is acceptable in marriage and parenthood. Until 1967, for example, laws prohibited marriages between white people and Black people, while throughout the twentieth century and into the twenty-first century, medical practitioners regularly sterilized people of color to limit procreation due to racist ideologies. These laws and routines are based in eugenics, which attempts to maintain white racial "superiority" by determining who could and could not marry or have children. And, as Jane Ward shows in her book *The Tragedy of Heterosexuality*, marriage is a key route toward white people's continued socioeconomic dominance, as marriage laws protect property and asset accumulation.[5] In the United States today, "normal" cis gay and lesbian marriage and parenthood were assimilated into this long-standing normative regime, placing white cis gay and lesbian married parents as adjacent to white cis straight married parents.[6]

Some of the white cis gay and lesbian people we talked with used homonormative logics, too, to do conflict work and stay in the family. As we'll show, some white gay and lesbian cis people and their parents use being in a long-term monogamous romantic relationship and having children to become normal.[7] But, as Max reveals at the end of the chapter, it is only those in relatively privileged race, gender, and sexuality statuses who can leverage this form of conflict work.

Percy Finds a Respectable Guy

Percy, a twenty-five-year-old white gay cis man, grew up in a Catholic home with his mom, Rosa, a fifty-four-year-old white straight cis woman, his dad, whom he describes as consistent but distant, and two "high-maintenance" brothers. Percy recalls his childhood relationships with his family were "really good;" his parents were supportive and allowed his independence. But when he was nineteen and came out to his parents their relationship took a turn for the worse. His mom, Rosa, like so many other parents in this book, got very angry; his dad didn't say much, but over time Rosa convinced Percy's dad that being gay was bad news. Ultimately, they both let Percy know "it was wrong and they needed to do something about it." As a result, Percy spent two years not talking to his parents.

Rosa explains her side of this story in her own interview. She agrees that she initially thought being gay was "very bad," explaining, "My first reaction was, after hearing him say that, 'Oh my God. My son is going to be made fun of, my son's going to have, you know, all of these terrible things that the world has against gay and lesbians,' it was just total fear at first. 'No, no, no.'" Rosa's reaction was also a function of her religious upbringing. She says, "I went right into the mode of okay, I am a fifty-four-year-old rural Catholic raised, Catholic educated. I had been told all of these things growing up that this was this and this was this and this is how we feel."

But things have recently shifted. "My relationship with my mother [is] better," Percy explains, and after a period of no contact he is now "open to the idea of fixing that relationship." Key to this shift, Percy thinks, was the entrance of Percy's new romantic partnership with Michael. "It's really changed her perspective of how things are going to be moving forward," Percy says. "They're realizing they see my investment in him" Percy explains, relieved, "and they see we cohabitate, we've talked of marriage, we've done all of these things, so I think they're slowly realizing that, oh, this is something that is permanent, it's not gonna go away." This change has taken some time and isn't complete—akin to the experiences of those we talk about in the rationale of growth in part I, with Percy saying, "It's an evolving process for sure. I think my mother has finally caught on that this is not anything that she can kind of sweep under the rug" because the romantic tie is visible. Rosa must accept him and his relationship or else risk another bout of estrangement from her son.

Rosa agrees that Percy's normal-ish romantic relationship with Michael helped her move toward acceptance. Percy being partnered to someone Rosa sees as a "respectable" partner with his own set of supportive parents showed Rosa how things could be. As a result, Rosa says, "I think our relationship is now stronger than it's ever been." Rosa, Percy, and Michael even went to therapy together, and in these sessions Rosa was embarrassed to realize that her rejection of Percy's sexuality caused him great harm. "All I could do was apologize to Percy and Michael."

Rosa sees Percy happy with a partner she likes, shifting her vantage point on her son's sexuality. "I think Michael and I have a pretty good relationship so far," Rosa says, and notes that Michael has a good influence on Percy. "I've seen Michael kinda reel him back in and I'm like, you are really good for him." Together, Percy and Rosa agree that they jumped from conflict work strategies—from the closet to the rug to education work. But ultimately, Percy demonstrating his committed and monogamous relationship through the work of normalization does the job to keep Rosa and Percy in good standing.

Kimberly Gets Married

Marriage is a pillar of respectability, a symbol of normalcy, and a key to accessing economic and social resources, as evidenced by the fervor with which gay rights organizations in the early 2000s fought for marriage rights.[8] Although marriage, like dating a significant other, can create more strain in parent-child relationships due to the increased visibility that comes with relationships,[9] several people we talked to explained their marriages helped relationships with their parents stabilize.

Kimberly is a thirty-one-year-old white lesbian cis woman who saw significant changes in how her parents treated her once she got married. Kimberly had a strained relationship with her parents, who divorced when she was about twelve, although the pair are back together now. Her dad, Howard (fifty-eight-year-old white straight cis man), was a "severe alcoholic" who has been sober for fifteen years. Kimberly recalls of her childhood, "When he was sober he was a great dad, but when he was not sober, awful dad." As a result of her dad's alcoholism and her parents' divorce, Kimberly lived primarily with her mom during childhood. Her mom was caring but wasn't particularly stable either, slowly "disappearing" into her own mental health and addiction battles and leaving Kimberly to feel like the primary parent to her two younger siblings. Kimberly oversaw getting her sister out of bed and ready for school whenever her mom was too hungover to do so.

After Kimberly became an adult, she moved to the Midwest for college, where she started dating a woman. For several years she hid her sexuality from her parents, but when this first serious relationship ended because her then partner couldn't take hiding anymore, Kimberly decided she wouldn't ever do that again to a partner. She wrote her parents a four-page letter about her childhood, telling them that she forgave them for their mistreatment and neglect. She ended the letter by disclosing her sexuality and explaining she was in a deep depression without their support. "I wasn't going to do that in my next relationship," she explains, and "I was actually ready to say goodbye to my parents." She went all in, telling them that while she forgave them for their neglect in childhood, not accepting her sexuality would be "the one thing I can't forgive, if you cannot accept me for who I am." Her mom called, crying and saying, "I love you and I'm here for you and that's not going to change that." Her dad called, too, but was "defensive." She explains why he struggled to apologize for the past and ignored her coming out, saying, "a lot of addicts have a hard time seeing the pain that they caused." Kimberly also notes he has some "internal conflict" about sexuality due to the religiosity of his twelve-step program. When her sister asked their dad what he thought about Kimberly's sexuality, he said, "I accept Kimberly, I love Kimberly. But the hard thing is that someone as kind as her and as loving as her won't make it to Heaven."

The dynamics started to shift with both her parents after her romantic relationship got more serious. Several years after coming out, Kimberly was preparing to marry her wife. But because of her dad's pushing her sexuality under the rug, Kimberly wasn't sure how he felt about her getting married and worried he might not come to the wedding. Howard was, indeed, troubled about the wedding. But, he did go, explaining, "I never saw a wedding quite like that. Never knew anybody that married someone of the same sex. Things change, though." He clearly is not pleased talking about the wedding in his interview, with his discomfort apparent in his reluctance to discuss the event. "Whether I accept it or not, doesn't really matter," he says, finally. "We love her and support her, and give her the opportunity to succeed and do the best she can throughout her life. Hopefully, it serves her well." Despite his ambivalence, Howard's going to the wedding was a pivotal moment for the pair, allowing Howard to publicly show his support and keeping their relationship intact.

This wedding was also a major turning point for Kimberly's mom, but in a different way. While Kimberly's dad was worried about the wedding, Kimberly's mom was excited. Kimberly explains, "I think my mom has been very excited over this past year for me to get married and me to be happy and wanting to be a part of that was a really big deal for her." Kimberly goes on to say that "during the wedding, she also pulled me aside and was like, 'I know I had a hard time with this at first, but I want you to know that I love you guys together and your relationship is really good.'" This was a huge moment for Kimberly, who had been wanting (and missing) her mother's full acceptance and love for so long.

Kimberly believes her getting married allowed her to fit within the norm of what children *should* do, allowing her parents to look past her sexual identity and accept her "good" relationship. "Their acceptance of my sexuality has taken a long eight years to get," Kimberly laments. And the fact that she had a "normal" wedding to a "respectable" person that her parents like made all the difference.

Wendy's Married with Children

For Wendy, a fifty-two-year-old white lesbian cis woman, the turning point of acceptance from her parents was not her wedding but her becoming a parent. To understand this shift, we had the opportunity to hear from not only Wendy but also her dad, Shane, a seventy-eight-year-old white cis man who identifies as straight and bisexual, and her mom, Cassandra, a white straight cis woman who didn't tell us her age. This gave us a unique vantage point into their family and the transitions toward acceptance.

Wendy grew up in a highly religious family with two brothers—one of whom lives in an assisted living facility due to serious health problems. Shane, her dad, traveled all over the world setting up missionary schools for a religious organization; he was gone two to three months at a time, often in remote areas that did not allow for consistent contact. The separation was stressful for Wendy because the two were extremely close—much more so than Wendy and Cassandra. Wendy went to religious boarding schools throughout their childhood, and it was in this context that she realized around age eleven or twelve that she might be a lesbian. Because of the repressive, explicitly antigay environment, she hid her feelings for a while out of fear, noting, "I was confused about my own feelings and so forth. So, because of my religious upbringing, I went through a period of time where I was suicidal, then I decided I'd try to be straight, try to date guys." It wasn't until college that Wendy fully realized she was a lesbian, and due to the antigay propaganda she had been taught, she had a breakdown. Her dad flew to her and stayed for a week, and Wendy told him about her devastating discovery. Shane recalls the conversation:

> She said "Dad, I am a homosexual." . . . Well, I, uh, immediately thought of all the challenges that could happen, wondered how in the world this

> would affect her. . . . She was crying, I was crying. And I took her in my arms and told her that "look, no matter what happens, you're my daughter, I love you, your mother loves you, and we will stick with you."

Wendy was relieved by his affirming response, but shocked when Shane told her that he too had feelings for people of the same gender and identified as both straight and bisexual. "To have somebody to talk to who was not condemnatory," Wendy, explains, "that turned out to be a very healthy good thing." Still, since Shane's job was in his religious organization, he told her to keep it a secret. "You know, I'm not happy that she's a lesbian. Simply because of all the trouble it will cause her."

While Shane's response was loving, even if repressive, Cassandra, Wendy's mother, had a difficult time processing this news. This was because Cassandra had always imagined Wendy marrying her childhood sweetheart and having children in the context of heterosexual marriage. Cassandra reports that when Shane told her Wendy's news, she was "upset, of course, because, you know . . . it was going to make a whole difference in our projection of her future, and our dreams of what she could be and everything." Relying on her own notions of what "normal" people are supposed to do, Cassandra says, "I had imagined she would get married, and have children, and be an engineer . . . those were the dreams that I saw crumbling when that happened." Cassandra's vision for Wendy's "normal" life filled with weddings and children and a respectable job was now ruined, she says.

Wendy recalls her and her mom's first conversation about her not being straight, with her mom saying, "'Oh no! This is so hard! It's gonna make your life so difficult.' So she was all upset and also, 'What will people think?'" Afterward Cassandra worked, like Shane, to get Wendy under the rug. According to Wendy, "She's like, 'Listen, your father's been able to be married all these years'" even though he is bisexual. "'Maybe you can make that work, too.'" This drama continued in the form of "a few heated conversations about that," with Wendy living under the rug for a few years at her parents' request. Wendy remembers Cassandra telling her, "Well, so long as you don't make me go to a gay wedding or have any gay babies I'll be okay."

Yet, despite Cassandra's fears, Wendy *did* get married and *did* have children with a woman. Cassandra did not want to be a part of their commitment ceremony, which took place before the legalization of same-gender marriage. At the time, Cassandra said she told Wendy, "I don't believe it's right. . . . I still think that it's the effect of sin in the world and that we shouldn't be celebrating it . . . this is like being born disabled, you know. It's a disability. And I can't see celebrating it with a wedding."[10] Much to everyone's surprise, however, Cassandra did end up attending the ceremony and actually stood in support. "They decided that they wanted to commit for life," Cassandra explains. "And they couldn't marry, of course, and so they had a commitment ceremony that was very much just like a little wedding." And twenty years later, Wendy's parents also participated in Wendy's legal marriage. Wendy thinks the weddings "helped bring them around," and Cassandra agrees.

Wendy's weddings allowed Cassandra to feel that her daughter is normal-ish, even if not straight. But Wendy thinks the event that really changed Cassandra's perspective was the birth of Wendy's daughter, Sarah. Wendy says that when her partner was pregnant, Cassandra "became an advocate and started telling everybody she had a granddaughter on the way." Wendy laughs remembering this, saying, "She had told everybody in her entire department at [a religious employer] that she had a new granddaughter and all of her colleagues had gotten gifts for her, just like they would for anybody else's grandbaby." Wendy was shocked at this response from her mom and her mom's colleagues. Her mom even insisted that Wendy and her partner "both come and show Sarah off to all of her colleagues. She really did an about-face. It was the grandbaby that did it. Really, it made her reassess her judgementalism."

Cassandra agrees that Wendy becoming a parent was a huge turning point, even suggesting her support was the reason they had a second child. Cassandra says that Wendy asked her, "What do you think? You think we oughta have another child, bring another child into the world with this conflicted family, and orientation and all?" Cassandra and Shane told them "'Yes, we think that you've been really good parents of the one you've got, and Sarah deserves a sister."

Ultimately, in their interviews, Cassandra, Shane, and Wendy all reflect that Wendy's marriage and parenthood were major turning points in Cassandra's acceptance of Wendy. Cassandra reflects on how much becoming a grandma changed her, saying, "They have been the best parents, and the children love each other dearly, and, you know, we look at each other and say, 'We debated whether this beautiful child should even be born?' She's a precious, darling thing. We love her to bits." By Wendy achieving a variation on Cassandra's dreams, the strain around Wendy's sexuality lessened. Doing the "normal" marriage and parenthood path won Wendy her mom's acceptance.

Max Can't Be "Normal" Enough

Only white cisgender gay or lesbian people in our study were able to access "normalcy" as a conflict work strategy in their relationships with parents. Deeply ingrained transphobia and essentialist beliefs about gender, as well as a focus on gay and lesbian equality with straights over the sexual and gender liberation of all, prevent some members of the LGBTQ community from achieving (or wanting to achieve) the status of "normal." The people of color in our study, as well as gender-expansive people and those who are queer, pansexual, or other sexualities, do not have the same access to "normalcy" even if they achieve the statuses of spouse and parent.

Rin interviewed Max, a thirty-seven-year-old Black queer GQ/GNC/trans person, in his bright and sunny downtown office.[11] Max grew up moving around the country due to his dad's position in the military, which he thought was "cool at the time." When his dad took extended trips out of the country, Max, his mom, and his older brother lived with their grandmother, who was Southern Baptist. Of their early life relationships, Max explains, "I was really close with my dad, and my mom and I struggled a lot. And that struggle often centered around my unwillingness to conform to gender norms." She wanted Max to play with girl toys and wear girl clothes, both of which he rejected. Kids in school also targeted Max because of his gender presentation and interests. "I was an awkward kid," he explains, "I think any kid who is struggling around conforming to gender norms is hypervulnerable to bullies." After high school Max moved away to the Midwest for college to get some space. But, around this same time, his parents separated (but never divorced), and his mom experienced some serious physical health problems. She needed extra help, and Max took that on, going back and forth from the Midwest to his mom's—about a seven-hour drive.

While overall Max had a fine relationship with both parents, things started to change when he came out as gay (an identity he no longer uses). When he told his dad this news over the phone, his dad had no response and hung up. Max thinks his dad reacted this way because "he was just so shocked" and felt "betrayed." After this phone call, he and his parents didn't talk for three months, a big change from their usual daily phone calls. At the end of this three-month period, Max saw his parents at a family reunion and thought, "This is awkward. I guess if we're gonna reunite, this is the place for it." Max's dad addressed Max's news at the reunion, saying, "You're Black, you can't be gay too. The world is just gonna be so bad for you." Max's dad draws on the fact that the United States is made up of a web of racist and homophobic systems of oppression wherein disadvantage amplifies if one sits in intersecting minoritized positions. While Max knows this critique is all too accurate, he wishes his dad could contextualize these broader fears within an accepting antihomophobic parent-child relationship. After this encounter, Max started setting boundaries on the relationship, especially when he visits. "I worked really hard to make myself financially independent so that I could be like, 'No, I won't stand for this. I won't be in this space, I'm out of here. I'll stay in a hotel if I have to.'"

His parents' reactions were much worse when he came out as trans and gender expansive. Max highlights how different it is to navigate coming out as trans/GNC/GQ than coming out as lesbian or gay—and why gender-nonconforming people do not have the same kind of access to "being normal" that gay and lesbian people do.[12] "When [my parents] meet someone's same-sex partner or something they're like, 'Oh okay, I get it. You have a same-sex partner just like I have an opposite-sex partner, okay. You all interact in a way that I understand, it's legible to me.'" Having a same-sex partner, he explains, allows people to approximate being normal. "And then for most of the people who I came out as queer to, the gender identity thing has been, 'Whoa, I just don't get that. I just don't get it. You're saying you feel . . . so you're a man?'" Max laughs as he says this, but he's deeply frustrated that his parents really don't get him.

Max goes on to emphasize how gender binaries are so taken for granted and ingrained that it requires that much more work to educate parents (see chapter 6)—and everyone else:

> So people just can't . . . because, you know, [gender is] such a ubiquitous sort of thing. It's so hard for them to think outside of that paradigm. . . . The hostility that I've gotten, it's because you sort of disrupted something that was clean and crisp in their world, you know? And it's just like, well, what does this mean for the way I see everything now? For this thing that's all around us, now it's not as neat and tidy as I used to think it was. And people get really hostile about defending their boxes, you know? Like, "No, these are my boxes, I'm only gonna have boxes, god dammit, my boxes." And I'm like, well, what if there are people who aren't in those boxes? You know? And I think for some people they're like, "You know, you're just confused."

Because Max "messes with people's boxes," he can't be "normal." In fact, Max is now married to a white cis woman and has a toddler—following the homonormative path of adulthood. But, unlike the others we talked to, Max's getting married and having a child did not earn him gold-star status in his family—it only ostracized him further. Given his parents' responses to his sexuality, Max knew that for him and his wife "to have a healthy marriage and for [my kid] to be a healthy kid that it was best to have limited involvement from my parents." Max's parents have been cruel to his partner and have ignored his child. This is unacceptable and has created a further rift. Now Max avoids going home and limits visits to once a year at most.

Today, during that once-a-year visit Max and his family stay in a hotel. "I have very strict rules around their engagement in my life. And since I've done that, I know it seems kind of sad, but it's not. It's very healthy." He is reflexive in this moment, continuing:

> The saddest part of it was when I was still so hopeful that things would change, then I would be like, "Oh yeah, come and visit, come and do this. It's gonna be great." Then it wasn't different, you know? Then that was like, "Okay, this is insane for me to think that at sixty, they're all of a sudden going to be different people." You know they're always going to be themselves, and the only person that I have power over is myself and the way I engage or disengage.

Ultimately, though Max stopped "trying to fix and repair those relationships. "And once I did that, then I was able to be like, 'Okay, I can just focus on having this positive thing here [my created family],' and sort of mediating where they converge."

While other people discussed in this chapter see their children as a bridge between themselves and their parents, the opposite is true for Max. Instead, Max keeps his child distanced from his parents because "I don't like for [my child] to be around them until they sort of figure out a way to embrace it. . . . And my parents can't even, you know, my dad is working on it, but my mom can't even wrap her mind around calling me Max. And it's been years. She uses my deadname. And then if I correct her, it starts a fight." Now, Max says, "I don't bother correcting her," and he does not work to counter her discursive aggressions. Max gave up on education work long ago, and being married with children does not allow him to go under the rug or become normal to fit in with his family. Instead, he remains on the outskirts of belonging with his parents.

Conclusion: Achieving Normal to Stay in the Family

While the people we talked to may not consciously find a significant other, get married, or have children to appease their parents, the privileging of so-called normal partnership and childbearing practices represents part of the arsenal keeping some parents and adult kids together. When education, closet, or rug conflict work fails, becoming normal is understood by some white cis gay and lesbian people as the glue that holds together their parent-child tie.

When learning their kid is LGBTQ, many parents initially talked about mourning the heteronormative marital and pronatalist future they had envisioned. For some parents, hearing their child is gay or lesbian means that they would not get to see that dream realized. However, of course, many lesbian and gay individuals do marry and do have children. For white gay and lesbian people, these acts make their sexuality legible and acceptable to their parents. This normalization might be seen as similar to what Amy Stone calls "comfort work," or the "navigations and strategies to reduce the discomfort of (presumed heterosexual) parents and reduce the disreputability to parents."[13] Becoming normal is clearly a way to make parents more comfortable with children's sexuality—intentionally or not.

Importantly, while normalization works to keep parents and kids bonded, there are limits to this approach. First, this strategy requires significant time and emotional energy from gay and lesbian adults to deal with their parents' rejection for long periods prior to normalizing events. Additionally, weddings and parenthood, while often providing individuals with a new opportunity for acceptance and growth from their family, also provide another opportunity for painful rejection from their family. Thus, it may be a risk to undertake this approach with the purpose of keeping the parent-child tie bonded.[14] Perhaps most importantly, this normalization strategy does not innately challenge the idea of what it means to be a "respectable" person. This limits the radical and liberatory power of LGBTQ politics, something shown time and time again is a consequence of the mainstream gay and lesbian rights movements.

And as we've discussed, *only* white cis gay and lesbian people in our sample maintained and repaired relationships with their parents through accessing the "normal" statuses. In using homonormativity, white cis gay and lesbian people gain family and societal acceptance, but they also uphold the power structure of monogamy, white supremacy, cisgender privilege, and capitalism together. Given the interwoven nature of these varying systems of oppression, it may be that people of color frame themselves as "normal" to their parents in ways that are different than the hegemonic normalcy of white marriage and parenthood found in this chapter.[15]

While the white cis gay and lesbian people in this chapter gained family acceptance by becoming normal, this normalization works to further marginalize those who sit outside of these privileged statuses, especially gender-expansive people of color, in terms of both family acceptance and broader liberation in society. As Marcus Hunter and many others discuss, race, gender, and sexuality are situated within interconnecting systems of oppression that are mutually reinforcing.[16] As such, the visibility of white cis gay and lesbian people accessing parenthood and marriage creates better parent-child ties only for a small sliver of the LGBTQ community, further marginalizing those who do not fit within this homonormativity. Given the broader systems of oppression that dictate respectability, white cis people's privileged gender and race statuses give them the ability to downplay their sexual identity and highlight their adherence to white cis marriage and parenthood norms, maintaining their place in the family.

9

Out of the Family

Anita, a twenty-four-year-old bisexual cis woman (who did not disclose a racial-ethnic identity), came to the Midwest for college after growing up in the mid-Atlantic region. Anita was one of the most tight-lipped of our interviewees about her childhood, noting before the interview even began that she did not want to talk about her mom, who died when Anita was young. Anita grew up an only child with her "controlling" dad, with whom she has an incompatible worldview.

Anita is just figuring out her sexuality now at age twenty-four. "I didn't really explore my own sexuality until later than most people probably do," in part because her dad taught her sex is "scary or dangerous; not something that is readily talked about." In addition, Anita hasn't told her dad directly about her sexuality because she knows he is homophobic. As a teen, when Anita would talk on the phone with one of her friends, her dad would confront her by saying, "That's what girlfriends and boyfriends do. You're not a lesbian," to which Anita responded, "Okay. How do you know that?" Her dad has other homophobic beliefs too. "When people were gay, he'd point it out; like it was a big deal. You know? He'd be like, 'Oh. This person, they're gay' or 'This person acts like this, so I think they're gay.'"

These kinds of homophobic comments constituted one more knot in a tangle of disagreements that caused Anita to cut her dad out of her life. "I stopped talking to my dad, September 2015, because I felt like the relationship was toxic to me," she explains. "He wasn't supportive, I didn't feel like it was bringing something positive to my life, . . . I guess I just view it like a cost-benefit analysis, and I felt like I wasn't really benefiting from the relationship at all." Her decision coincided with a physical move to the Midwest for college. "I was, like, 'Okay. I'm already moving to a new place, I'm getting a new phone, I might as well just do it now.'" She goes on to explain that the distance made her realize "how dysfunctional my conversations were with my dad. How he would just spend a long time talking about himself," and she didn't feel like she had to put up with it any longer. "I guess just me being more mature and more emotionally aware, psychologically aware of myself—more of an adult. It made me realize how he's not an adult. So, it was like, 'Okay. Why? This relationship isn't doing anything for me. I'm more mature than he is.' I don't go to him for advice." So she cut him out.

Anita did *think* about staying in a relationship with her dad despite his rejection and lack of support, but only because of the power of compulsory kinship. She explains, "It was still a hard decision, obviously, and I think I felt a lot of external pressure, I guess. Just the idea of a daughter not talking to her father anymore is, I think, frowned upon." Anita had always "grown up with people saying to me like, 'Oh, you're so lucky that your dad is here' because your mom passed away.' So, I guess I felt . . . there's this pressure in society like, 'Family's very important,' and [I got pressure] from people that knew me thinking more positively of my dad than I did." This pressure—what we call compulsory kinship—is so strongly felt that she considered staying in this bond even though she didn't benefit from being in touch with her dad. But, ultimately, Anita does not give in to the sociocultural pressures of compulsory kinship that tell her what family should be. Anita is coming to terms with the power of compulsory kinship and her decision to step outside of it—to cut off her dad. Her own questioning of why she should keep this damaged bond has allowed her to take a step back from her father, creating long-lasting distance from the compulsory nature of this tie. And, for Anita, this was a great decision. As she told us, "Wow! I have to worry so much less."

When the Bough Breaks

As discussed in part I, compulsory kinship is an unrelenting force rationalized through notions of closeness and love, growth, and uniqueness, and bolstered by the conflict work (from being in the closet, to engaging in education, to using the rug, to becoming "normal," as described in part II). We want to take some time here to consider a few of the people who were able to break free from their parents, mostly fathers, at least for a time.

Family estrangement is the "physical distance [or] a lack of emotional intimacy, [by] one or both parties [who consider] the relationship to be unsatisfactory."[1] Estrangement is relatively uncommon but deeply life-altering, with estimates of its occurrence ranging between 2 and 6 percent of parent-child ties.[2] This wide range reflects a variety of definitions of estrangement, since there is no legal "divorce" and thus no clearly defined end of a relationship between parents and adult children.[3] Some scholars consider estrangement to be little to no contact (i.e., physical estrangement), while other researchers consider estrangement to be a lack of affection and emotional intimacy (i.e., emotional estrangement or disengagement).[4] Estrangement has also been measured on a continuum, varying by the quality and degree of contact, disengagement, emotionality, and reciprocity.[5]

While destructive to the parent-adult child tie, estrangement from parents can be a key resilience strategy used by LGBTQ individuals to recover self-esteem and mental health in response to family homophobia, biphobia, and transphobia.[6] For example, Amy Stone and colleagues (2019) shows that for some transgender and enby adults, being estranged from parents eases adult family trauma, including the damage done by parental gender misrecognition. This strategy, Stone suggests, is more likely to be deployed by Black and Latinx people as well as those with economic strain in childhood and adulthood.[7]

Anita, whose story is presented at the beginning of this chapter, is one of only a small number of people in our study who intentionally cut off her relationship with her parent. Her story is powerful in its complete, intentional, and discernible rejection of compulsory kinship. A few other people had similar approaches to their dads—discussed in the next section of this chapter.

However, others we talked to have enacted periods of estrangement only temporarily. In presenting these cases, we show how estrangement can actually be a way that compulsory kinship is reasserted.[8] When adult children cut parents out, this is often only temporary, with some people resuming their relationships at a later date. As such, we argue that for these LGBTQ adults, periods of estrangement paradoxically reassert compulsory kinship.

Dad Doesn't Uphold Compulsory Kinship

The father-child relationship is notoriously less stable than the mother-child tie due to the gendered organization of parenting. As such, children are more likely to be estranged from fathers than mothers in the United States today.[9] Several people we talked to discussed how their father-child relationships have ended, and as with Anita, their stories allow us to see the powerful force of compulsory kinship.

Jeanette and Maureen never had a relationship with their dads. Since their fathers did not participate in parenthood when they were young, as adult children Jeanette and Maureen do not feel the need to uphold or begin this relationship. And, their estrangement stories have more to do with the nature of fatherhood in America than with children's gender and sexuality. Jeanette, a twenty-five-year-old white lesbian cis woman, knows her dad's name, but they don't speak. Her brother talks to him, she says, "because they used to do stuff when my brother was a kid." But Jeanette has been to her father's house maybe two or three times in her entire life. The most recent, and she hopes last, time was because she needed his info for a FAFSA application when she was trying to get financial aid to go to college. At that point, he wanted to start a relationship, but Jeanette simply said, "You know, this doesn't change anything. Like, I still don't know who you are. And . . . you know, you are not . . . my dad." Maureen, a twenty-three-year-old Black gay/lesbian cis woman, never knew her dad, who divorced from her mom when Maureen was a kid. She explains that their relationship had "little to no existence." She remembers the ages at which she saw him—six, eight, twelve, seventeen. Her dad was never dependable, and "He never showed up. I stopped hoping." They don't talk today.

But most others we talked to *had* a relationship with their dad at some point only to subsequently dissolve it. Isobel, a white twenty-three-year-old queer cisgender woman, grew up in Appalachia and now lives with her enby spouse. Isobel was always close to her mom, April, a forty-five-year-old straight white cisgender woman, while her dad was aloof and abusive when Isobel was growing up. April describes her husband as "very cruel, very, very abusive," adding, "I spent most of Isobel's childhood as the buffer between the two of them. And I'd try to make him go easier on her. I would try to make her, 'Just do this so we can please your dad.'" As a result of this environment, Isobel and her mom became incredibly close—and still are, talking daily—while Isobel and her dad have no relationship.

Isobel's parents separated when she was fifteen and divorced when she was eighteen. She was outed to her mom by students at her school around the time of her parents' separation. Isobel says her mom, April, had a "hard time" with Isobel being queer, telling her, "You're going to hell . . . you're just sinning." As April explains, "I didn't want her to be lesbian, I wanted her to just be normal, just be straight. Everybody else is straight, why do you cause all this aggravation and trouble." Yet April is more understanding now due to some serious education work. Isobel explains, "I think we've learned to work together. . . . I think she's learned to work with me and who I am." In turn, April agrees, saying, "I just went to her, and I told her, 'I love you, and I don't care if you're gay, straight, whatever.'" But there was a big caveat: "We have to hide it from your dad."

And hide it they did. That is, until Isobel was eighteen. When her dad found out, he said, "'Oh, you're gay. You're not my daughter anymore.

I don't want to see you again.' He punched a wall, he was, 'I don't want anything to do with you,' and he said something like, 'God hates lesbians.'" Isobel pauses her story and then says with without emotion, "I don't talk to my father anymore." Not only was he rarely present in her life, she says, but when he was, he was emotionally abusive—something she only now realizes after years of therapy as an adult. "Even before I was out," she says, "even before he knew I was gay, he was just not there for me. I never wanted him to be around because he was just always mad, always yelling. I was really glad when he was gone." His reaction to her sexuality was the last straw in their relationship. April is happy for Isobel's strong stance, although she feels guilty for allowing him in her daughter's life at all:

> She tells me that she hates him, he never treated her right. He was very cruel to her when she came out as lesbian, he was just completely awful. She said if he would have apologized to me, admit what he did wrong, she might consider having a relationship with him, but she says he's dead to her and she doesn't accept anything from him.

April is totally fine with the pair's estrangement, saying of her ex, "By this point I'm just like, I don't care what you think, she's eighteen now, there's nothing you can do." Her dad is out of the picture, and the whole family has a restraining order against him; his reaction to Isobel's sexuality was one more reason to cut off contact.

Isobel has no regrets. "At this point I'm just glad that my dad is out of my life," she says. "That's where I'm at. We just don't have a relationship. I don't usually even say I consider him my father. I usually just don't say that I have a father . . . he wasn't a good dad and then I stopped talking, so he's not a dad at all anymore."

Cut You Out, but Let You Back In

There are others who cut their parents out for a period but eventually let them back in. Tabitha is a twenty-nine-year-old Black gay/lesbian cis woman who has lived with her parents in a large metro area her whole life, save three and a half years of estrangement. Rin and Tabitha sat in a coffee shop, across the room from where Tabitha's mom, Deanna (who is a sixty-three-year-old Black straight cis woman), was being interviewed. Despite the public place, Tabitha was not shy, talking at length about her mental health, her sexuality, and her troubles with her parents.

Tabitha, an only child, has serious mental health problems and was diagnosed with bipolar and borderline personality disorders; Deanna also mentions that Tabitha was diagnosed with schizophrenia in third grade. These mental health diagnoses are a backdrop to how Tabitha handles her parents' homophobia. It is clear that while her sexuality is part of the conflict with her parents, Tabitha also deeply struggles with mental health issues that complicate her relationship with her parents tremendously.

Tabitha and her parents fought for years around her sexual and gender identity and about her being an atheist. "They would not let me be me. And live my life and make my decisions," Tabitha explains. "It was always the three of us moving as one. And they didn't understand that I don't like that. I don't operate that way. That's not what I'm about." Tabitha, like many others, thinks her parents' negative response to her being gay is due to their religiosity and her parents "being old school southern Black folk," who believe "being gay is also a no-no."

The big break in compulsory kinship came when Tabitha legally changed her name in 2009 to better reflect her identity and to assert her independence. "They didn't accept it. I didn't talk to them about it for that reason, because I knew they were going to try and talk me out of it. And so it was kind of like the day that it was official was when I told them. They don't understand why I did it." A huge fight ensued. "So that was the straw that I—and I was so pissed and this fight got so heated that this dog was cowering behind the couch, shaking." She says, "That was when I knew I had to go. Because I am violent. I have hit my parents before, and so I had to leave, because I knew something bad was going to happen. And they had kicked me out before. And with a fight like that which was so heated and 'fuck you, bitch' and this and that, I knew they were going to kick me out. So I felt like I beat them to the punch."

Ultimately, living with her parents was too restrictive. "They just—I felt like they wouldn't just let me be me and do what I wanted to do and make my decisions with my life. So I had to go to a super-extreme." For Tabitha, this meant leaving home—and even leaving the state—to allow Tabitha "to prove that, you know, I love you guys, but I'm not living my life for you. I'm living my life for me." She rejected the rationale of love that upholds compulsory kinship to end this tie.

Deanna, too, narrates this final blowup, saying that Tabitha went "crazy." Deanna remembers Tabitha saying, "You don't trust me, you don't like me. You don't love me. You don't understand me. You're messing with me, I hate you. You know, I was—I was—I was her worst enemy." But Deanna insists this is not true. When Tabitha legally changed her name, Deanna was "very sad," not really understanding why she did this, and was confused and hurt that she didn't want to keep her given name. But at the same time, Deanna explains, "I knew she was a lesbian before she did," insisting she loves Tabitha for who she is. When Tabitha left, Deanna says, "I was devastated. I was devastated. I absolutely was heartbroken. I cried all day. I just stopped living . . . she's my only child, and what we did and what we've been through and all this, and then for someone to hate me that much, to hate me so much that she'd actually pack up and leave and leave the state?" Deanna was especially distraught that Tabitha called her only twice in the years she was gone. "It was anger when she left, it was anger when she called, it was anger when she was gone."

Tabitha returned three years later. Her mom was so hurt, she hesitated to let her back in. But when Tabitha told her she was homeless, Deanna opened her house back up. She says her husband facilitated this reconciliation, saying, "'That's our daughter,'" drawing on the rationale of uniqueness that purports once a child, always a child, in chapter 4, "'she deserves a second chance.'" Tabitha now lives with them again, but things have changed. "They're not as parental as they used to be. When I first got back, they were still pretty mom-and-dad clingy. But now, we're all adults. And—so that's nice." After this, Tabitha's parents worked to respect her sexuality, but "only because they have to." This resulted from their estrangement when "they realized that I'm good either way with or without them. And the same cannot be said for them about me." Tabitha says, "They want me in their lives so much to where they would accept bad behavior or, you know, whatever. I'm good either way. If you can accept me and love me for who I am, cool. If not, I don't need you sticking around in my life regardless if you love me or not." To this day, though, Tabitha still doesn't feel they understand her. "I don't feel like they ever understood me, and it doesn't matter how you feel. I'm still gay. I'm still an atheist. So you can either love me or hate me, but either way, I'm still going to be a gay atheist. So you can get on board with that or not." Tabitha is grateful "they're finally on board with it."

Tabitha can live with or without her parents. But she did come back, suggesting that in the end, compulsory kinship, as well as resources provided through family, is a force to be reckoned with. Her mental health diagnosis makes the conflict around her sexuality (and nonreligiosity) even more challenging, often making what starts as calm discussions roll into full-blown arguments. Still, her returning to her parents suggests a commitment to the parent-child tie, even if buttressed by estrangement.

Our final story of cutting out a parent (but letting them back in) comes from Brad and his parents. Rin interviewed Brad, a nineteen-year-old white gay trans man, and Emma interviewed his mom, Gina, a fifty-one-year-old white cis straight woman, in a crowded coffee shop.[10] Brad, his mom and dad, and two siblings lived together until Brad's parents divorced when he was eleven—a divorce caused by Brad's dad's physical, emotional, and financial abuse, leaving an already troubled father-child relationship hanging by a thread. "He can get really angry at times," Brad says simply but sadly.

During his freshman year of high school, Brad started to realize that he was a boy, crystallized in the moment he got his first menstrual period. "It was awful," Brad says, explaining that this moment affirmed his gender identity. But Brad's transition is complicated by his serious mental health diagnoses, including borderline personality disorder, unspecified bipolar disorder, and schizophrenia. He has tried to commit suicide more than a dozen times and was incarcerated for almost a year after attempting to physically harm his sister. Through it all, his mom, Gina, has been his safe haven. Brad emphasizes the love and support his mom gives him regarding his mental health and his trans identity, which took a bit of education conflict work similar to what we illustrated in chapter 6. Gina says, "I think we're very close. A lot of it is because I have been his strongest advocate once I came around and realized this wasn't just another phase he was going through or something he was doing to get attention. I still don't think I really understand it, but it's real to him, so it's real to me."

Things are drastically different with Brad's dad. Although the divorce in his childhood allowed visitation with his dad, Brad cut that off for a couple of years because of his dad's continued abuse and his rejection of Brad's trans identity. As Brad recalls, "And when I told my dad [I am trans] he got so violent, the police was almost called." Brad cut his dad out for a couple of years because of this response. But now he talks to his dad "a little bit." Why?

Brad explains the feeling of being fatherless changed his mind, reflecting: "I don't want to be without a dad. I went like that for a couple years and I didn't like it." Brad draws on the rationale of uniqueness, described in chapter 4, to explain his decision, noting simply that he doesn't want to be without a father figure no matter the quality of that relationship. As a result, Brad went from cutting his dad out to slowly exploring a relationship, even it is just superficial and even if it is damaging. For Brad, it is important to *have* a dad, even if his dad does not live up to the standards or hopes of what a dad is supposed to be.

Conclusion: Out of the Family?

It is through the rejection of compulsory kinship—even temporarily—that we can see its true strength. The people we talked to recognize the severity of cutting off their parents, but they do so when the relationship reaches a point where they can no longer reframe positive experiences as more salient than negative ones. Estrangement was far more common with dads than moms, as dads already are more likely to have a precarious relationship with their children due to the structure of parenting and the norms of masculinity that disconnect men from emotional closeness with their children in the United States today.

Estrangement was used across racial-ethnic categories, but we observed notable differences in how estrangement was done across race. Black and Latinx people experience serious strains and stressors due to the systems of racial oppression in the United States today. To buttress their resources and identities, Black and Latinx people are more likely to have consistent and sometimes daily contact with family networks, as well as larger extended kin networks, than white people. These networks serve as significant sources of emotional, financial, and instrumental support, so estranging oneself from a key part of these networks—parents—comes with significant social and financial penalties.[11] As Stone, Nimmons, and Davis show in their study on LGBTQ family estrangement, Black and Latinx people who are already in marginalized or economically insecure positions due to a white supremacist capitalist society may have fewer points of support if they choose estrangement.[12] And across racial-ethnic categories, those with fewer economic resources rely more on kin networks, with parents at the center, than those with more economic resources, also indicating the centrality of class and resources for familial experiences.[13] These needs likely draw individuals back into the parent-child tie, as well as uphold the centrality of the family, even when those ties are strained.

The strength of compulsory kinship, especially through the rationale of uniqueness we discussed in chapter 4, continues to be felt even during periods of estrangement, influencing decisions and reinforcing the importance of parent-child ties. Those who leave parent–adult child ties consciously go against the grain of societal expectations. But when parents fail miserably at their end of the intergenerational deal, children feel more comfortable breaking their unspoken promises as well.

Conclusion

A Less Compulsory Kinship

Throughout this book, we make the case that kinship between parents and their adult children is compulsory. We develop the concept of compulsory kinship to call attention to the fact that most people stay in parent-child relationships not by individual choice alone but because of intense social forces that constrain and guide these relationships. This is the case even for LGBTQ adults, who experience more strain and rejection from parents on average than do cishet people.[1]

In part I, we show *why* most of us remain tied to parents even after childhood. We demonstrate that the "natural" and inevitable connection between parents and adult children is in fact created and sustained by the sociocultural force of compulsory kinship. Then we show the specific rationales that LGBTQ adults use to keep in line with compulsory kinship and justify the continuation of strained ties to parents. In the rationale of *love and closeness*, white and Asian women and white gender-expansive people emphasize being close to and loving parents as a reason to stay bonded, even when there is serious strain and discord. The rationale of *growth*, used especially by people of color and gender-expansive people, reveals the power of the promise of progress in maintaining parent-child relationships. The final rationale of *uniqueness* was used most readily by LGBTQ adults of color to explain that they must stay in this relationship because the parent-child tie is irreplaceable. Each of these rationales allows people to explain *why* they maintain the parent-child tie—or adhere to compulsory kinship—even when the reality of this relationship may not come close to the ideal family bond.

In part II, we show *how* interviewees adhere to the norms of compulsory kinship through a type of family work we call "conflict work." Conflict work makes visible the serious effort of staying bonded—effort that is normally de-emphasized or made invisible by prevailing assumptions of an abiding tie between parents and their kids. When parents reject a core part of who their child is—their gender or sexuality—significant work must be done on the part of the LGBTQ adult to maintain that relationship. While it may appear that the continuation of the parent-child tie is *natural* or *inevitable*, the examples in part II clearly show that in fact immense work is put in by LGBTQ adults to maintain that tie. The *family closet* was used by white and Asian LGBTQ people as a way to hide their sexuality and avoid parental rejection altogether. Once out, LGBTQ people taught *gender and sexuality school*, where LGBTQ adults, especially gender-expansive people, worked to educate parents on their gender and sexuality. If education didn't work, LGBTQ adults across gender, sexuality, and race-ethnicity went *under the rug*, never speaking about being LGBTQ after coming out. And, when these approaches failed, white cisgender gay and lesbian adults were able to *become normal*, adopting normative and desirable statuses of married (with children) to get parents to accept them. Finally, a few LGBTQ people across gender, sexuality, and racial-ethnic identities moved *out of the family* when the conflict work is not sufficient to keep this tie bonded, although this move was almost always temporary.

Altogether, this book shows that compulsory kinship is a major sociocultural force in our lives. People deploy broader socioculturally endorsed rationales to explain these continued but strained relationships and use conflict work to stay in the boundaries of compulsory kinship. But after diving so deeply into the operation of compulsory kinship in this book, we now want to give some insights into how we can we make kinship less compulsory.

The compulsory relationship between parents and children might sound like a great deal to some—especially those with healthy parent-child ties. Of course, the parent–adult child tie *can* result in a life full of positivity, support, and kindness. But for many people this is not the case. We believe if parent-adult child relationships aren't good for everyone, then parents' primacy in our social structure and in adult children's social identities *must* be questioned. Even though there are some "good" parents, the fact that "bad" ones have so much power should provoke us to radically rethink our societal reliance on this kinship institution.

Today, children need parents to survive and thrive in both childhood and adulthood—with few good alternatives for care and belonging provided through social or governmental safety nets. And children see their parents as central to their own self-identities—the source of their emotional health and sense of who they are. But what if your parents don't have the means or desire to help you in adulthood? Or, what happens when your parents ignore you, reject you, or are verbally or physically abusive? What if you just simply do not get along? Due to compulsory kinship, these ties persist, regardless of quality. The parent-child relationship is so central to contemporary society that it is difficult to imagine an alternative.

Applying Adrienne Rich's words about compulsory heterosexuality to kinship is helpful to advance our critique of the primacy of the intergenerational bond in the United States today. *In the absence of choice, adult children will remain dependent on the chance or luck of particular relationships and will have no collective power to determine the meaning and place of parents in their lives.*[2] Without real choice, adult children cannot decide on the primacy of parents in their family.

What would a setup that is not so reliant on parents look like? Some alternatives have been suggested by feminist, queer, and Black, Latinx, and Indigenous activists and scholars.[3] We draw on this vast scholarship to offer two possibilities: restructure society to be less reliant on parents or create healthier parent-child ties for all.

Restructure Society So Adults Can Be Less Reliant on Parents

To have a society with less compulsory kinship, we need to unroot parents as a *necessary, only, and ideal* basis of care and identity when children are adults. So, how do we do that?

We need to create *an ethic of care regardless of familial bonds*. What this means is that everyone regardless of age or family network structure should have a sense of belonging and identity, alongside emotional, practical, and financial help, from their community and their local, state, and federal governments. A system built around an ethic of care would give people a broader and more secure backdrop of support that is not based on biology or de facto "family" relationships.[4] In doing so, we would take the *compulsory attachment to parents* out of the equation.

In making this shift, we would first need to decouple adults' financial and practical needs from parents. We haven't focused on the role of financial support in maintaining parent-child relationships because other research already does that quite well.[5] Instead, our aim was to explore the more insidious sociocultural forces that keep parents and their adult kids together. But here we want to call attention to how reducing financial dependence between parents and kids is an *imperative* first step if we want to diminish the sociocultural compulsoriness of kinship. Take the example of who gets to take paid and unpaid leave from work to care for another human. In the current model, the state-defined "family" is primary, and under FMLA provisions you can only obtain leave to care for a parent, spouse, or child.[6] In this system, if someone in your neighborhood or friend group or even a person who is unhoused on the street is sick, you cannot legally take time off from work to care for them. A society built around an ethic of care would allow *anyone* to take leave from a job to care for *anyone else* in need.

But we can (and must) go further. Instead of linking health care and health insurance access to the "right" kind of kin (read: biological or legally recognized relationships such as spouses, parents, or children), we all could be able to add *any* person to our health insurance that we choose regardless of their status as "kin." Even better, we could all have health insurance regardless of employment or relationship status. And, rather than automatically setting up survivorship rights to go to a "next of kin," wealth at death could be redistributed to those most in need in society. We could make college free, allowing adults to be able to afford an education without having to rely on parents or massive student loan debt.[7] To make it possible for more people to get good jobs, we could increase the number of free apprentice training programs. We could support affordable housing so that people can live on their own away from parents if they choose to. We could institute a living wage that would allow people of all occupations and jobs to survive independently, far above the poverty line, without parental help. On the grandest level, we could divest from capitalism and create a system that isn't reliant on wage labor—which is inherently unequal and makes some people more reliant on their parents.

All of these changes would divert adult children's financial reliance on parents and allow adults to feel freer to leave their parents—to break free of compulsory kinship. These are just a few ways to decoupe care from kinship. But the point is this: we need to *create a wider net of social and economic supports* so parents aren't a primary source of resources.[8]

But as we've shown in this book, even if parents don't help their adult children financially, compulsory kinship keeps parents and kids bonded for life. We next must go beyond the practical and financial to *reorient our sense of self and community away from, or at least not so dependent on, parents*. Once we decouple the financial support system from parents, we can tackle what this book is really about: the sociocultural imperative to situate parents at the center of family.

In this new approach, we would not place our sense of self—our identity of who we are and what we are here on this planet for—on being a parent or child. If being a parent or a child isn't our main identity marker, people could create other identities outside of parent and child to develop a more holistic sense of purpose and belonging—like lover, friend, roommate, aunt, helper, neighbor, colleague, mentor, apprentice, or community member. In doing so, people can build a more resilient sense of self that isn't inextricably tied to parents, and parents could allow their adult children to be independent and even estranged without losing their own sense of belonging, purpose, and identity. This might mean that when our parents fail us—when we cannot get our needs for belonging and acceptance met through these ties—we have a much wider range of social actors who can step in and help us meet our needs. This would mean that adult children do not need to deploy endless conflict work to stay in relationships that aren't working. Instead, we could leave those relationships behind without huge social and personal costs. As such, we could create a world where a plethora of social ties are routes to self-discovery, identity, understanding, healing, community, and belonging, rather than one that insists that parents are almost always at the center of who we are and what we do.

Some communities are already revolutionaries at developing alternative forms of community, belonging, and identity-making.[9] Black adults have long created fictive kinship networks to bolster community and resources, in part due to adaptation to racism that we have discussed throughout this book, including the legacy of slavery.[10] But people of all racial-ethnic groups create fictive kin, even if they also uphold the normalcy of bio/legal kinship with parents.[11] Such fictive families draw on other types of kinship models for belonging and identity to create a system of love, support, and stability. They intentionally make the broader notion of kinship more flexible by not relying on the hegemonic ideals of what "family" should be—rejecting the racism, (cis)sexism, and heteronormativity built into the normative kinship system. Some families even engage in "kin reinterpretation" that redefine a distant biological relative as closer than a parent, some rename a parent-child relationship as "like siblings" when that bond is nonhierarchical, and some interpret friends and colleagues as primary kin.[12] Similarly, LGBTQ people have famously created families of choice to develop networks of support, love, and belonging not received from their families of origin.[13] As such, queer people and people of color have already laid the groundwork for widening the scope of identity formation, belonging, and support above and beyond family of origin.[14]

While some would lament reducing the power of parents, we believe de-privileging parents at the center of "the family"—and by default the center of who we are, what we value, and who we associate with—our lives can become much richer. We would then have a more diverse range of relationships that aren't necessarily linked by procreation, biology, or the debt of being raised. In this model, care *between people, and the interpersonal identities people inhabit, are diversified.* As such, parent–adult child relationships would be "maintained by a consensus between the individuals involved and can be relinquished at any time"—decidedly not compulsory.[15]

In the place of the traditional parent–adult child tie could be a society where we're freer to organize resources, identities, a sense of belonging, and support in creative ways that make sense for more people. People lament being beholden to the family—you can't choose your family, so the people in this book say. But if the meanings placed on parents and children are diminished or altered, maybe we could *choose* which social ties we have and what we expect of each other. New, more equitable forms of community and belonging that can care for all would emerge. There are great models that start us on the path of decoupling parents as *the* site of identity and belonging. We think that the more widespread and sanctioned alternative families, fictive families, and families of choice can work to restructure how we receive and give care, love, and belonging in society rather than just biological, compulsory, and hierarchical parent–adult child ties, the freer we will all be.

Restructure How We Parent to Create Healthier Parent–Adult Child Ties

Maybe forming a system of care and belonging beyond parents is too radical—or seems impossible. So, instead, we could also think about reorganizing the family—and the parent-child tie—to ensure it is a safer and more supportive place for all. To do so, we need to rework what it means to be a parent of an adult child.

So-called experts and laypeople alike will tell you what a "good" parent to an adult child is, but sociologists know that what it means to be a good parent is culturally constructed, classed, racialized, gendered, and changes over time.[16] If we don't restructure society to allow adults to be less reliant on parents economically, socially, developmentally, and for a sense of identity and belonging, we can still reframe the relationship between adults and their parents as more equal and voluntary.

First, we need to shift away from the ubiquitous expectation that parents will always have "their" adult kids in their lives, and that these ties will always be hierarchical. To do so, we need to reinvent a culture of kinship that is free of compulsory forces, placing parents and their adult children as equals in a relationship that is mutually agreed upon and able to end without massive repercussions. In short, we need to "redo" what it means to be a parent and an adult child.

To this end, we need to do a better job of providing parents the emotional, psychological, and intellectual resources and cultural norms that allow for being in relationship with adult children in a loving, supportive, independence-inducing and trauma-reducing way. This will also take a major cultural shift in what we think of as parents' role in the lives of their adult children. While current norms of parenting give parents—especially mothers—many rules for how to be *good* parents to adult kids or for how to help their adult kids be *successful* in our modern society, what is missing is equal access to emotional, intellectual, and psychological resources such as therapy and counseling to help parents with their *own* emotional needs as their children gain independence. We need to be less worried about exactly how to parent, or what skills or techniques make the best parents, and instead learn the basic tools of how to be a compassionate human who can accept their adult children *as equal adults* who deserve to be respected for exactly who they are.

We need more tools—both individually and societally—to help parents learn how to deal with their own emotions around an adult child no longer being under parental authority. We need to help parents negotiate a person who once was their child but is now an independent person from them. We need to create a new framework of parenthood to help parents deal with their own disappointment and emotions around adult children making decisions for themselves—especially when these decisions do not fall in line with parents' desires. We need to change our culture in important ways to *reshape* parent–adult child relationships, removing parental subtle and overt control over their adult children and place less emphasis, importance, and expectation to continue the same dynamics present when children are minors.

With this sort of reimagining, we can have mutual, equal, voluntary, and healthy parent–adult child relationships—and of course we can have parent–adult child relationships that end in healthy ways. Part of this shift is the tackling of homophobia, transphobia, biphobia, and other anti-LGBTQ cultural ideologies that restrict parents' ability to have mutual and supportive relationships with their LGBTQ adult children. We need to support gender and sexuality freedom in children—from childhood to adulthood. We need to teach parents about sexuality and gender acceptance and activism, and of course we need to eradicate sociocultural and individual LGBTQ-phobia.[17] In a sexual and gender liberatory society, all sexualities and genders are not only tolerated but *celebrated*. This is why helping people be better people to their adult children will be a solid step toward a safer world for all LGBTQ people.

Where Do We Go from Here?

The compulsory nature of the parent-child tie binds us all, but maybe it doesn't have to. We offered some possible alternatives as a starting place for thinking about a more just and caring society that is not built around the forced ties between parents and their adult children, but we are sure our readers will be more adept at creating a better vision given the chance. We imagine an environment where parents and children could consciously choose to stay in relationship—or not—and where either option is a good and life-affirming choice. Because of the stories of the people we wrote about in this book, we truly believe a society less tied to compulsory kinship—one that relies less on compulsory kinship rationales and conflict work that keep parent–adult child ties together—could be a better place for us all.

ACKNOWLEDGMENTS

We want to thank several people who made this book possible. Our biggest thanks goes to the LGBTQ people who opened up their lives to us. We hope that we did justice to your stories, both collectively and individually. We are humbled by your candidness and vulnerability and have taken great care with your words and your stories. So many of you expressed to us your hope that sharing your stories can help other LGBTQ people find their way. If this book has such an effect, it is entirely because of you. We also thank the parents of our LGBTQ adults who were candid and forthcoming even when it was uncomfortable to do so.

In addition, we thank our core research team members, Alex Kissling, Korrie Johnson, and Lauren Gebhardt-Kram. They were part of our project from the start, helped us conceive this study, helped us recruit participants, and conducted interviews with us. We also thank Lawrence Stacey, Jess Goldstein-Kral, and Sam Dubin, who helped with the project at its inception. As a team, we created a project that we are proud of, and this book is in large part due to your collaborative work. Thanks, too, to other Ohio State University students and faculty in the Department of Sociology who have discussed bits and pieces of this book over the years and who have provided an invaluable intellectual community from which this project emerged and developed, including but not limited to Doug Downey, Brandon Moore, Chloe Dunston, Cindy Colen, Hollie Nyseth Brehm, Kara Young, Kara Waalkes, Kait Smeraldo, Korie Edwards, Kristi Williams, Luther Young, Meredith Zhang, Rachel Dwyer, Sarah Hayford, Townsand Price-Spratlen, and Wes Wislar. We presented components of this project at the American Sociological Association meetings and published heavily revised parts of this book in the *Journal of Marriage and Family* and *Social Problems*; in doing so we received helpful comments from numerous editors, reviewers, and colleagues who facilitated the progress of this book. We also thank Cathy Hannabach at Ideas on Fire for the index of this book.

Finally, we want to thank our editor at NYU Press, Ilene Kalish, as well as assistant editor Sonia Tsuruoka. Ilene believed in this book years before any words were written on the page. She encouraged and guided us throughout the process, and we are so grateful that her vision aligned with our own. Thank you for believing in us and our work.

RIN'S ACKNOWLEDGMENTS

I could not ask for a better co-author than Emma, who is a true collaborator in every sense of the word. Emma pushed this project forward with her clear thinking, theoretical depth, unparalleled analytical skills, and clear and compelling writing. Throughout this process, she helped me develop and grow as a scholar, and I am forever grateful for her partnership on this project.

Cati Connell, Clayton Howard, Daniel Snider, Danielle Bessett, Kara Young, Liz Lee, Megan Reid, and Mieke Beth Thomeer gave invaluable feedback at various parts of this process. I'm grateful for their keen eyes and perspectives that made this work better. Thanks go to the Department of Sociology and the Institute for Population Research at Ohio State University, which provided funding to pay interviewees for their participation (P2CHD058484), and to the Department of Women's, Gender, and Sexuality Studies for providing an intellectual environment that challenged and supported me during periods of this book's conception and writing. Thanks also go to the National Institutes of Health, which supported me during periods of writing this book (1R01AG069251-01A1), and special thanks go to Deb Umberson, who has been a never-ending supporter of me and my work since the time I entered graduate school so many years ago. I also thank my child's daycare teachers, Jean, Josey, and Beverly, who have very literally made the writing of this book possible.

It is not lost on me that this is the place in the book where the author thanks their family. Given that this book tries to denaturalize "the family" and loosen the parent-child tie imperative, this presents an interesting opportunity to note my own investment in, and divergence from, compulsory kinship. Several members of my given family deserve acknowledgment and appreciation, and rather than emphasize their titles and roles (e.g., mom, dad, sibling), which we ultimately try to deemphasize in this book, I'd like to name them here as a collective group who have influenced who I am and how I think on the deepest levels: Aaron, Chris, Clara, Dianne, Jane, Jim, Jeff, Joe, Marcus, Mina, Nora, Rebecca, and Vera. Within all of the complex context of given family and compulsory kinship that span the decades of my time on earth, I thank this group of people for your special place in my life.

My chosen family are abundant, and for that I am incredibly grateful. So many dear friends are invested in my life and this book: Amanda, Andrew, Catherine, Cindy, Clay, Danielle, Erynn, Janean, Joachim, Kara, Lara, Liz, Matt, Megan, Mieke, Monica, Nicole, Peter, Rick, Tan, and many others. You all asked about my work, listened to my ideas, and told your own stories of family that greatly influenced my thinking. Of perhaps highest importance in this category of chosen family is Sarah, with whom I shared an eleven-year partnership spanning my twenties and early thirties and an abiding twenty-year friendship that continues today. From our relationship came the inspiration for this book. For years we braved going "home" together to see our parents, complete with painful encounters and tears. I remember many conversations in which we asked each other, "If our parents don't accept us, why are we still going to see them? Why do we still talk to them?" I spent the last decade trying to understand these questions, and part of my answer is this book. Out of hardship came greater understanding, and for that—and for your true and forever friendship—I am so grateful.

The linchpin in my chosen family is Danny—whom I'd like to address directly. It is an honor to share a home and so many days with you. You read this book more times and more closely than anyone but Emma and me, and in doing so you made this piece of work clearer and more accessible. You also helped give voice to my thoughts, discussing my ideas for hours and days on end with unnatural patience. Your companionship—both in writing this book and in the hundreds of other ways you provide it—is invaluable. And you are an amazing chef, parent, and gardener—comforts I am certain this book could not have been written without.

Finally, I dedicate this book to Nico, who is about two years old at the time of this writing. Writing this book with you in my life has given me a new perspective on the parent-child tie. When people ask me how I would feel if you didn't want a relationship with me once you became an adult, I acknowledge I would be sad. But, you don't owe me anything—even though the forces of compulsory kinship say otherwise. When you become an adult, I'd like to recognize my own historical power in dictating our relationship, and purposefully reassess and reformulate our tie together. I'd like to imagine a time when adult you and I consciously choose to stay in relationship—or not. We would assess: What do we like? What do we not like? Do we want to keep our relationship going? If yes, what can we do to make it better? It is with you in mind, Nico, that I imagine a world where parent–adult child relationships are more mutually decided and on equal footing. Sure, the forces of compulsory kinship would likely rear their head, and I'm likely naive for thinking I might be able to sidestep them. But maybe we could create something new, too.

EMMA'S ACKNOWLEDGMENTS

I want to begin by thanking my co-author, mentor, and adviser, Rin Reczek. Rin has given countless hours to my development and confidence as a scholar. I will always be grateful that they have been such a core part of my support system in graduate school and that I've gotten to collaborate with them on this book and other publications.

Thank you to so many of my friends and colleagues in graduate school. To Elizabeth and Jake, who have been constant sources of support, friendship, and jokes: whenever I hear the songs "Unwritten" by

Natasha Bedingfield or "Bring Me to Life" by Evanescence, I will think of our writing times throughout graduate school. To my Zoom working group during COVID-19, Elizabeth Martin, Jake Hays, Sadé Lindsay, Melissa Alcaraz, and Laura DeMarco, thank you for helping me feel connected during a year that has been really hard for so many. To Lesley Schneider, for providing baked goods and lending me great books!

Thank you to those I met as an undergraduate student who have remained an integral part of my life: to my undergraduate adviser, Mary Tuominen, who first taught me to see myself as a researcher and scholar. To Jill Gillespie, who talked through the decision to apply to graduate school with me, and who helped me go to my first conference the summer after graduation. To my mentor, Natalie Pariano, who is a source of compassion and creativity always. To my friends and travel partners, Kristine Mallinson and Gary Fleisner.

To my partner, Aaron Butts, your belief in me, your constant support, and the home we share are all so meaningful to me. Thank you for being my partner and my friend. Graduate school would have been so much more difficult without you there always encouraging me, talking through ideas, and helping me laugh easily and often.

When writing these acknowledgments, I googled "how to write acknowledgments" because I'm overwhelmed by the number of people I'd like to thank. Ironically, because of the main argument of our book, the first that came up was "family members (spouse, children, parents)"—compulsory kinship in action! While writing this book, one of the things I've grappled with is the idea of family as compulsory, but also as so important to my understanding of myself and my life. To my family, I want to thank you for showing me how family can shift and change over time. To my mom, Cindy, and my dad, Shannon, for your love and care over the years. Thank you for helping me to grow, for giving me my love of reading and sarcastic humor, and for fostering creativity and fun in our household when I was growing up. Thank you, Dad, for all your visits to see me in graduate school and for your consistent love of photography, British television, and me. Thank you for finding your husband, Wade, and bringing another loving person into my life (who has taught me many great board games). Thank you, Mom, for all of your phone calls, advice, and edits you have given on work I've written. Thank you for our quilt weekends and our movie nights, for talking through my anxieties with me and for always making me laugh. All three of these parental figures have played a huge role in my life, and I'm proud of the family we have. These new understandings of family have changed me for the better and are a core part of why I now dedicate myself and my work to critiquing and helping to dismantle sources of oppression. Thank you to Isabel and Molly, my sisters, whom I've had the privilege to see grow up these past years. Isabel, you are one of the strongest people I know, and Molly, I hope to one day be as cool as you. To Eric, Laura, Phil, and Myles, getting to be a part of your life in Columbus these past six years has been one of the best gifts. Phil and Myles, I'm already thinking of how you can come visit when I have to eventually move!

METHODOLOGICAL APPENDIX

STUDY APPROACH

The stories we've told in this book are a small selection of narratives from our larger interview sample. The people we introduced in these pages are exemplars from our data: those we felt best captured the themes of the book. To provide a broader picture of the project, we want to share a bit more about who we are, who we interviewed, what we asked people, and how we came to our conclusions.

In this study, we aimed to understand the sustained relationships between LGBTQ adults and their parents. Recognizing that previous literature focused on either LGBTQ adolescents and their parents, or LGBTQ parents with young kids, we wanted to focus on LGBTQ *adults* and their parents. This gap seems especially important given recent attention to emerging and young adulthood as a precarious life stage. If adolescence is precarious for LGBTQ kids, what happens after kids become adults? What is the nature of intergenerational relationships as children seek to become independent?

We collected survey and qualitative data between 2015 and 2017 in a large Midwestern city and its surrounding metropolitan and rural areas. This site was chosen because research on LGBTQ populations has predominantly been conducted in the coastal urban areas, missing a perspective that focuses on Midwestern LGBTQ lives.[1] In the Midwest, 3.6 percent of adults identify as LGBT; an estimated 20 percent of all LGBTQ individuals live in the Midwest, emphasizing the importance of studying LGBTQ experiences in this region.[2] This sample may reveal something particular about LGBTQ adults in the Midwest and their parents because experiences and understanding of LGBTQ identity vary by place,[3] in part due to geographic differences, including religiosity, levels of acceptance of LGBTQ identities, and access to LGBTQ resources.

We interviewed seventy-six LGBTQ people and forty-four of their parents (of forty children as a few of our respondents had us interview both parents). All interviews were one-on-one interviews to allow for each individual's story without the other generation's input. Originally, we intended to interview only LGBTQ young adults whose parents would also be interviewed in order to get "both sides" to the intergenerational story. But we quickly realized this was a mistake. While most interviewees were "out" to their parents, as we show in chapters 5 and 7 many avoided the topic of being LGBTQ at all costs in order to preserve the relationship, making them less likely to participate in a study for which parents being interviewed was a requirement. Thus, we interviewed some adult children without also interviewing their parents. As a result of this research strategy, we use parents' interviews throughout this text to provide context for adult children's narratives, but we have not included every LGBTQ person's parents in the study. We only contacted parents with children's approval in order to protect children's privacy. Some of the children who did not want their parents interviewed had highly conflictual parent-child ties, and therefore our parental data on the whole are skewed toward more positive parent-child ties than is the case for the child sample on the whole.

Interviews averaged about ninety minutes but spanned from forty-five minutes to three hours. Interviewees received a twenty-dollar gift card as an incentive for participating. The majority of adult children interviews occurred in person—either at team members' offices or in coffee shops. A small percentage of adult children's interviews were conducted over the phone when geographic distance or lack of transportation was an impairment to in-person interviews. More than half of the parent interviews were conducted over the phone because many parents lived more than an hour away from the interviewers.

Interviewees were recruited through a variety of methods including, most commonly, flyers distributed throughout the city center in LGBTQ+-friendly locales and a booth at local Pride events; a number of interviewees were recruited through social media and participation in specific transgender and gender-expansive events or via snowball sampling from previously interviewed people. The recruitment materials explained that researchers at a university were doing a paid study of LGBTQ+ adults and their parents and provided contact information, with an email address, to request more information. A main priority of recruitment was to have a racially, economically, gender, and sexually diverse sample of LGBTQ+ adults; thus interviewees were initially screened from a wider pool of interested subjects based on diversity in gender and sexual identity, age, race-ethnicity, and socioeconomic status. In particular, we declined interviews with white, gay/lesbian, or cisgender men and women as well as those with advanced degrees after we had the current number of each group represented in the sample.

DEMOGRAPHICS

We show the demographics of our sample in table A.1. Overall, the demographics of our sample match the demographics of the Midwest. We wanted to talk to LGBTQ adults of different ages due to drastic changes in the lives of LGBTQ people across the past century. We interviewed LGBTQ people between eighteen and sixty years of age, but most interviewees are between the ages of eighteen and forty, with an average age of thirty-one. Thirty-six percent of the sample identifies as gender expansive (e.g., trans, GNC, enby/GNB, or GQ). We include demographics of the parents in table A.2; the parent sample is disproportionately white straight cis women, and in part because of this limitation we do not focus on the parents in this book.

We interviewed people of diverse class backgrounds in terms of education, income, wealth, and occupation. About half of the sample is what we consider socioeconomically disadvantaged in that they have a high school education or lower, have an income at or below the poverty line, or are in traditionally blue-collar occupations. A few people experienced incidences of being unhoused, consistent with research showing LGBTQ—especially trans people—have much higher rates of being unhoused than cishet people.[4] Due to systemic and interpersonal racism and the resulting precarity of LGBTQ people of color, and because people of color have often been left out of research on LGBTQ families, we specifically aimed to hear the stories of LGBTQ Black, Latinx, Asian, Native American and Indigenous, and other nonwhite people, who make up a quarter of our sample.

Pseudonyms were given to all participants to protect anonymity, and we use the pronouns the participants indicated in their interviews. We kept the factual integrity of each interviewee's story. However, some details were too specific and were changed or left out to protect participants—including names of people, towns, and workplaces, as well as dates and other very specific identifiable information.

RESEARCH TEAM'S POSITIONALITY

The research team consisted of five researchers who conducted the interviews, with each interviewer acutely conscious of our own race, gender, sexuality, and class during their interviews. Rin is white, queer (sexuality), and enby, and Emma is a white, cisgender, straight woman. The other team members are a Black, cisgender, straight man; a white, queer, cisgender woman; and a white, cisgender, straight woman. We tried to match interviewer-interviewee's race and gender. But regardless of these choices, we remained conscious of how race-ethnicity, gender, and sexuality informed the type of data we received, often writing about these dynamics in our field notes after the interviews. For example, we found in the interviews that many of the LGBTQ people assumed the person interviewing them was LGBTQ, even if the interviewer was a straight person. When asked, interviewers always told their identity, but when not asked, they often kept personal information to themselves. This likely created a unique interview situation that shaped the data collected. For example, forms of "insider" knowledge were presented to straight interviewers; interviewers often had to ask for clarification on well-known LGBTQ references. While interviewers asking for clarity on a concept or event helped get at the underlying meaning of a word that otherwise would not have been uncovered, it can also be alienating and othering to LGBTQ interviewees.

Additionally, when there was a mismatch in the race of the interviewee and interviewer, power dynamics of a white interviewer interviewing a person of color, alongside a lack of shared cultural knowledge, inevitably shaped the interview data collected. Rin recounts one interview with a Black trans woman who laughed with what Rin perceived as good humor throughout the interview at how white Rin sounded. This interviewee took great care to explain terms she felt Rin would not understand as a white person. While this was helpful for Rin, this likely was taxing for the interviewee and without doubt shaped the topics and depth of the interview.

Interviewer-interviewee race, gender, sexuality, and class dynamics shape not only the data that are collected, but also their interpretation. Rin and Emma analyzed the data in stages, with Emma sorting the data into large "topic" codes (i.e., conflict with parents, the closet) and Rin conducting more fine-toothed interpretive analyses that make up the themes of this book while regularly consulting Emma. As such, there are important issues to consider regarding representation in both Emma and Rin writing this book, including, most important, our interpretations of the data as white anti-racist feminist authors. We consulted with scholars of color about our interpretations of the narratives presented in this book and have worked to reference and call upon the immense knowledge of scholars of color throughout this book to enhance our interpretations. In particular, we worked throughout the book to draw on scholars of color to facilitate our analyses, to privilege an interpretation of the lived experiences of people of color within the historical and contemporary systems of racism and colonialism, and to situate our own privilege as white authors. However, ultimately this piece of work was written by two white people and is thus limited by our white perspectives.

We also must consider our gender identities as they relate to the interpretation and presentation of our interviewees' stories. While Rin and Emma have long studied gender and sexuality in both academic and popular texts and worked to privilege the trans and other gender-expansive stories in this book, ultimately the book is shaped by the authors' genders. Emma is cis, and Rin is enby. Even as enby is often placed under the trans umbrella, enby experiences can be quite different than those of individuals in other trans categories. Moreover, Rin is a white sociology professor, which provides a very privileged class context in which to be enby, including job security and a relatively supportive work environment. Rin discussed the findings in this book at length with trans friends and colleagues, including one Black trans person in the sample of people interviewed with whom Rin keeps a close social connection, but ultimately the interpretations and decisions were made by us as authors.

We hope we did justice to the people whose stories are represented in this book. We recognize our interviewees' articulation of themselves, and our interpretation of their stories, may differ from our readers' experiences and interpretations. We hold this tension as part of the beauty and complexity of qualitative research.

TABLE A.1. Demographic Information on Adult Children Sample

	n (%)		n (%)
Sexuality		**Household income**	
Gay or lesbian	39 (51%)	$1–$49,999	34 (45%)
Queer	13 (17%)	Above $50,000	33 (43%)
Bisexual	12 (16%)	No response	9 (12%)
Multiple categories selected	9 (12%)	**Gender**	
Other (pansexual, fluid, straight)	3 (4%)	Cisgender	47 (62%)
Age		Transgender	18 (23%)
Average	31	Genderqueer/gender nonconforming	6 (8%)
Range	18–60	Multiple gender categories selected	3 (4%)
Education		Not disclosed	2 (3%)
Some high school	1 (1%)	**Race**	
High school graduate	7 (9%)	White	54 (71%)
Some college or technical school	16 (21%)	Black	10 (13%)
Current student	11 (14%)	Asian or Pacific/Islander	3 (4%)
College graduate	20 (26%)	Multi-Racial	2 (3%)
Postgraduate or professional	18 (24%)	Hispanic or Latinx	2 (3%)
No response	3 (4%)	Native American or American Indian	1 (1%)
		No response	4 (5%)

Total number of respondents: 76.

TABLE A.2. Demographic Information on Parent Sample

	n (%)		n (%)
Sexuality		**Household income**	
Straight	40 (91%)	$1–$49,999	11 (25%)
Queer, bisexual, or fluid	4 (9%)	$50,000–$99,999	17 (39%)
Age		$100,000 or above	15 (34%)
Average	59	No response	1 (2%)
Range	42–77	**Gender**	
Education		Cisgender man	10 (23%)
High school graduate	8 (18%)	Cisgender woman	34 (77%)
Some college or Technical School	11 (25%)	**Race**	
College graduate	12 (27%)	White	40 (90%)
Postgraduate or professional	12 (27%)	Black	3 (7%)
No response	1 (2%)	Hispanic or Latinx	1 (2%)

Total number of respondents: 44.

LGBTQ ADULT IN-DEPTH INTERVIEW GUIDE

Today we're going to focus on your relationship with your parents, but we will also talk about your siblings, extended family, your romantic relationships, and children. We're going to talk about you as an adult later, but first, tell me about what your life was like growing up.[5]

A. Childhood

1. How were your relationships with your parents (and other family members) growing up?
   a. Living arrangements, general description of closeness, conflict? What kind of housing and economic situation were you in?
   b. Who are your siblings? Who else did you live with? What were your relationships like with each person you lived with or consider "family"?
   c. How has your relationship with your parents changed as you became an adult?
      i. Were you close? What does that mean to you?

   d. Did you/do you live with your parents as an adult? Get that story.
   e. Did you get a job or go to college? How did that change your relationship?
   f. Did you have any significant family deaths in your childhood? Who were they, and how did it impact your health?
2. What was your health like? [mental health, health behavior; any major illness/injury, stress in your life]
   a. How did your parents or siblings try to shape your health and health behavior (e.g., smoking, drinking, exercise, food, sleep)? Did it work? Did they ever make your health worse?
   b. What about mental health? Have you ever had periods of depression? [follow up with suicidality if they bring it up]
   c. What was your parents' health like growing up? Any major illness/injury?
3. LGBTQ specific
   a. How do you identify your gender and sexuality? How has this changed over time?
   b. Are you out to your parents? Siblings or other family members? Tell us this story.
   c. How have your relationships changed since you came out? How has coming out been good or bad for your relationship?
   d. If not out, why not? What do you expect the reaction will be?

B. Adulthood

Now I want you to talk about today.

1. General parent-child tie
   a. Describe what your relationship is like now with your parents. How has it changed over time? What about your relationships with your siblings? How do you, your siblings, and parents interact now and over time?

b. Did you have any significant family deaths in your adulthood?

c. Closeness.

  i. How close do you feel to your parents now? How close do you think they feel to you? Is this different from how you would have answered this same question when you were younger?

  ii. Define being close.

  iii. Which parent are you most like? Why? How does that affect your relationship?

  iv. How would you like this relationship to be now? What is your ideal relationship with your parents? What prevents it from being the ideal?

  v. How do you think your relationship impacts your overall mental and physical health?

  vi. Are you close to your siblings? Explain.

d. Conflict.

  i. What do you fight about with your parents?

  ii. What are ways in which you resolve conflict?

  iii. Are there times when you've felt especially distant from your parents?

  iv. How does conflict affect you?

  v. Did this ever cause depression or stress? If so, how did you deal with this?

  vi. Have you ever considered ending this relationship? Have you ever stopped talking to your parents?

  vii. Do you have conflict with your siblings? Explain.

C. *Significant others: partners, spouses, siblings (that weren't covered above), extended family, grandparents, friends, children*

Is there anyone else especially important to you that I missed? Get the story on these relationships from childhood to adulthood—quality, conflict, closeness, estrangement, overall family dynamics, health and health behavior.

PARENT IN-DEPTH INTERVIEW GUIDE

I want to spend the bulk of the time today talking about your children. We're going to talk about your parent-child relationships, the types of conflict you've had, when you feel close to them, and both your and their health from the time they were kids to today.

A. *Parent-child relationship dynamics*

Who are your children? [Get all info, how old they are, order, etc. Make sure to get step/half/adopted kids as well, and any children who passed away.]

1. General dynamics: What your children do and where they live? How often do you see them?
    a. Did your child live with you from the time they were born until they turned 18? What was your relationship like growing up?
    b. Did your kids leave the nest? Have any of your children lived with you since turning 18?
        i. What was that like for you? What was it like for them? If still in home, describe the relationship.
        ii. How did your daily routine change?
        iii. How did your health change at this time? Major illness/ injury?
2. Closeness
    a. How would you describe your emotional closeness to your children? Theirs to you? How does this make you feel? Do you think you'd agree on this question? What makes you think you are close? Define this for me.
    b. How has your sense of emotional closeness changed over time? Are there/have there been times when you feel/felt especially close to your child?

c. Do you ever try to make your children feel better about themselves or a situation? Is it successful? Do they ever try to make you feel better? How so? Does it work? If not, do you want them to? What would this look like?
d. What do you love most about your relationship with each child? Which aspects of your relationship with each child come with ease?
e. Do your children rely on you for emotional support? What does this look like?

3. Conflict
    a. What types of things do you fight about with your children?
        i. How has this changed over time? Have major life events played a role in this change?
        ii. How often do you argue? What are ways in which you resolve conflict? Are there times when you've felt especially distant from your children?
    b. Are conflicts stressful? How do you deal with this stress?
    c. Is there anything you'd like to change in your relationship with your children?
    d. Have there been conflicts that ever involve all the children?
    e. Have there been conflicts that involve a particular child?
    f. Are there aspects of your relationship with your children you'd like to change?
    g. How do you deal with the stress of conflict with children? How does this affect your health behaviors?
    h. If more than one child:
        i. Which child do you feel closest to, today and over time?
        ii. Do you feel like you are fair in how you treat your children?
        iii. Which child do you go to with your problems? Why?
        iv. Are there things you'd prefer to do, or talk about, with one child and not the other?

4. LGBTQ specific
    a. Are any of your children LGBTQ identified? If so, how do you know?
    How did this affect your relationship? How has their identity affected your relationship? Your family?
    b. If not, how would you feel if one of your children were LGBTQ?

B. Parents

1. Are your parents still living? What was your relationship like throughout their life?
    a. When do you feel especially close to your parents? What are sources of conflict?
    b. Do you caregive for your parents? How so? Get that story. Financial, emotional, practical? What does this look like? How much time do you spend? How do you feel about this caregiving?
        i. Did you ever feel like you had to choose between your parents and your children in terms of time and resources? How do you make this decision?
    c. Have your parents ever cared for you? Do they ever impact your health?
        i. Did your parents ever have any other influence on your health and health behavior?
2. What are/was your children's relationship with your parents? Do they ever provide care for your parents?

C. Significant others: partners, spouses, extended family, grandparents, friends

Is there anyone else especially important to you that I missed?

NOTES

GLOSSARY

1 See Stryker (2008) for details on the history of the term "transgender."

2 Adapted from C. Reczek, 2020. This list does not include other important terms that were not used by respondents, including, for example "aromantic" (i.e., someone who experiences little to no romantic attraction), which is a distinct identity from asexual.

INTRODUCTION

1 Other types of caregivers can and do provide care to minor children—grandparents, siblings, extended kin, strangers, organizations, and governments. Many other care structures have existed besides the parent-child bond throughout history and across geographic place.

2 Offer & Fischer, 2018.

3 The letters of the acronym LGBTQ do not directly include many other marginalized sexualities, genders, and sexes (e.g., enby, pansexual, asexual, intersex, agender). We use this term to speak broadly of the entire group of gender and sexually expansive people and acknowledge and validate the presence of multiple genders, sexes, and sexualities within the LGBTQ umbrella. We use a more specific term for each interviewee throughout the book.

4 Meadow, 2018; Travers, 2019; Brainer, 2019; Ocobock, 2013; A. L. Stone, 2020.

5 Robinson, 2020; Moore, 2011; K. L. Acosta 2010, 2013; Brainer, 2019; Decena 2008, 2011.

6 The title for this book, *Families We Keep* is a companion of Weston's *Families We Choose*. This classic work is part of the inspiration for ours, and we place our work in conversation Weston's famous concept of "chosen families."

7 "Outsider-within" was coined to explain how Black women are both a part of but also distinct from the dominant culture due to their subjugated race and gender statuses. As a disadvantaged group, they have the ability to see multiple vantage points not readily seeable by the privileged. We apply this concept to queer people, recognizing that Black straight cis people experience unique forms of disadvantage relative to LGBTQ Black, Indigenous, and white people (P. H. Collins, 1986).

8 P. H. Collins, 1999, p. 85. As part of a Black feminist theoretical approach, Collins shows us how Black women have a unique standpoint from which they

understand the world around them based on their outsider-within position in a particular social setting. In this article, Collins calls out race, gender, and class as key statuses; Collins's later work *Black Sexual Politics* (2004) adds sexuality as a vector of identity that shapes standpoint.

9 In this book, we focus on those relationships that involved parents who were homo/bi/queer/transphobic. Although most of our interviewees talked about intensive conflict with parents due to their gender and sexuality, some interviewees had loving, supportive relationships with their parents. We do not suggest *all* relationships between LGBTQ adults and their parents are negative or harmful.

10 i.e., a person whose sex and gender assigned at birth match their current sex and gender.

11 Robinson, 2020.

12 Rich, 1980.

13 Pronatalism refers to both official governmental policy and social norms that pressure people to have children.

14 "Family" is used to denote many relationships in our culture, but the parent-child tie is considered by many as the basic unit of family.

15 Weston, 1997, p. 34.

16 A version of part I and the concept "rationales" is discussed in Bosley-Smith and Reczek (forthcoming) in the journal *Social Problems*. However, the data and analyses presented here are an expanded version with greater depth and many alterations.

17 Erickson, 1993, 2005.

18 A version of part II and the conflict work concept is discussed in Reczek and Bosley-Smith (2021) in the *Journal of Marriage and Family*. However, the data and analyses presented here are an expanded version with greater depth and many alterations.

19 The original quote, which references compulsory heterosexuality, reads, "In the absence of choice, women will remain dependent on the chance or luck of particular relationships and will have no collective power to determine the meaning and place of sexuality in their lives." Rich, 1980, p. 659. We discuss Rich and the concept compulsory heterosexuality in Chapter 1 and in the conclusion.

20 Abrego, 2014; Chatters et al., 1994; Gill-Hopple & Brage-Hudson, 2012; Taylor et al., 2013; Weston, 1997; For a review, see Furstenberg et al., 2020.

CHAPTER 1. COMPULSORY KINSHIP

1 Kane, 2012.

2 Dow, 2019; Stacey, 2021.

3 Hartnett et al., 2018; Pillemer, 2020. Estrangement implies a relationship was intact at some point; those who have never met a parent (most often fathers) are not included in the estrangement categorization.

4 McLanahan & Jacobsen, 2015.

5 P. L. Berger & Luckmann, 1966.
6 Fingerman et al., 2012; Doepke & Zilibotti, 2019.
7 The notion of men and women as "opposites" has long pervaded Western thinking on gender. This, of course, is a false notion. There is no "opposite" in sex or gender; instead, this frame is used to emphasize supposed differences between genders, to reify the false gender binary, and to prop up heterosexuality as the only viable option for sexuality.
8 Baxter et al., 2009.
9 Bulanda, 2011.
10 Nelson, 2006; Sarkisian, 2006.
11 Notably, not all parents are, or have historically been, given the same legal and social rights due to their race-ethnicity, social class, biological parentage, and sexuality. In fact, the parent–minor child bond can be, and often is, broken when the state via social workers or other child "advocates" frame certain parents as unfit. White middle-class parents are assumed to be "good" parents on account of racialized and classist notions of proper parenting. In contrast, Black, Latinx, Indigenous, and working-class parents are often judged harshly for parenting practices that do not fit within the white middle-class ideal.
12 The notion of "roles" has fallen out of favor in sociological thought because of the common interpretation of roles as static and unchanging. We contend that while certainly there are parent and child roles, we prefer the idea of sociocultural norms or forces, which provides us with more leverage to discuss how people understand their institutional, social, and cultural contexts.
13 Scott, 2013.
14 Cherlin, 1978; Gerth & Mills, 1953; P. L. Berger & Luckmann, 1966.
15 The normative pillar of institutions consists of ideas around duty, expectations, values, and norms and is based around obligations to other people. Behavior is shaped by the perceptions of other people and is subject to policing and punishment (i.e., accountability). Normative systems are broader and more deeply held internal beliefs that guide what should be desired or worked for, as well as the proper way to go about meeting those goals. This group of theorists includes Émile Durkheim, Charles H. Cooley, and Talcott Parsons. These normative systems can be seen as providing stability and community within societies, such as in Parsons's work. A different set of theorists focus on the cultural-cognitive pillar. These theorists—such as Clifford Geertz, Peter Berger, Paul DiMaggio, and Irving Goffman—focus on how the external world is interpreted through cultural frames. Cultural-cognitive scholars often focus on the role of symbols, meanings, and frames in interpreting and interacting in the social world. See Scott, 2013.
16 Bulanda, 2011. We can see the "doing" of family in the example of marriage. People are expected to legally marry, and marriage is expected to take a normative form of monogamy, coresidence, shared resources, enduring love, and child-rearing. In effect, engaging in these practices—and sometimes altering them and

shifting them to suit one's needs—is how people "do" marriage. Although historically only heterosexual marriages were legal, same-gender marriages have recently become part of this family institution. The fact that almost everyone in the United States, even LGBTQ people, wants to marry, and that the vast majority of people do actually marry at some point, reflects the strong social forces around marriage that are veiled as a purely individual choice. Yet, when people question the primacy of marriage—like many queers, feminists, lesbians, and Black women have been doing at least since the 1970s—these critiques are often rejected because they challenge modern notions of the primacy of romantic ties. Like marriage, intergenerational ties are also institutionalized. We could draw on the same logic and language to explain the relationship between parents and children. People are expected to stay bonded with parents, and that bond should take a normative form of consistent contact, coresidence until age eighteen (and sometimes beyond), shared resources, and enduring love. The fact that almost everyone in the United States, even LGBTQ people, stays in these bonds reflects the strong social forces around the parent-child tie that are veiled as a purely individual choice. Yet, when people question the primacy of the parent-child tie, these critiques are often rejected because they challenge modern notions of family-of-origin primacy.

17 Fenstermaker & West, 2002; Thompson & Walker, 1995; C. West & Zimmerman, 1987.

18 Sarkisian, 2006, in a response to Nelson, 2006, p. 804, defines "doing family."

19 Nordqvist, 2017; Nelson, 2006; Sarkisian, 2006.

20 Naples, 2001, p. 33.

21 Gallagher, 2003, 2007.

22 Cherlin, 1978; Cherlin & Seltzer, 2014.

23 D'Emilio, 1983, p. 474.

24 Parents can decide what school a child goes to and dictate children's participation in sports and music in school as well as religion outside of school. Parents have a legal right to their child's earnings and an expectation of physical custody of their child.

25 While circumcision is seen as normative in the United States, this is not the case globally (see Gollaher, 2001). For a primer on intersex genital reconstruction surgery, see Davis, 2015.

26 For a primer on the history of childhood, see Zelizer, 1985; L. Stone, 1979.

27 In 1938 the Fair Labor Standards Act was passed, ensuring that children be given a safe and reasonable working environment that did not impede their education.

28 Zelizer, 1985. Parents are given the legal obligation to provide food, housing, and other life-sustaining goods and services to young children—rather than the previous arrangement in which children helped provide food and services to their family. These legal and financial obligations were codified in what is referred to as the parental rights doctrine. This doctrine can be traced to the early 1920s. For

example, in 1925 the US Supreme Court ruled in *Pierce v. Society of Sisters* that an Oregon state statute forcing parents to send their children to public schools (as opposed to private schools) encroached on parents' rights to make decisions regarding their children's education. The legal and financial authority of the parent took further hold in 1944 in the US Supreme Court case *Prince v. Massachusetts*. The Court ruled, "It is cardinal with us that the custody, care and nurture of the child reside first in the parents, whose primary function and freedom include preparations for obligations the state can neither supply nor hinder." Such legal decisions solidified the authority of the parent over the state in fulfilling children's basic needs (George & Baldwin, 1997, p. 158; for a full summary of these court cases, see Skinner & Kohler, 2002).

29 Zelizer, 1985, p. 57; L. Stone, 1979.

30 Morgan, 2002.

31 Hays, 1998, p. 54; Lareau, 2011.

32 There has been unrelenting violence toward Black children, most famously and horrifically in the brutal lynching of fourteen-year-old Emmett Till in 1955 and more recently the murder of Trayvon Martin in 2012. This is alongside efforts to prevent Black children from integrating into the better-funded white schools, through first legal and then implicit segregation. Black, Latinx, and Indigenous children are disproportionately more likely to be removed from their parents' home by state agencies than are white children. In the Obama, Trump, and Biden administrations (although most famously in the Trump administration), Latin American and South American families coming across the US-Mexico border have been subject to family separation, with distraught infants, toddlers, and young children being separated from their parents and placed in the custody of the US government or white parents. Given the legacy of the racist, colonial enslavement of Black, Latinx, and Indigenous people, as well as nationalist policies that adultify migrant children and children of color, those marginalized based on skin color, nationality, and immigrant status are disproportionately at risk of having their parental power usurped by the state (Onwuachi-Willig, 2017).

33 Shedd, 2015; Goff et al., 2014; Bernstein, 2011; Mitchell, 2008.

34 Also see Lopez 1999.

35 There is a rich history of research on Black, Indegenous, Asian, and Latinx alternative kinship models (Chatters et al., 1994; Gill-Hopple & Brage-Hudson, 2012; Nelson, 2020; Taylor et al., 2013). This body of work de-emphasizes the nuclear two-parent married family. Several studies on global parenthood, such as Lan's *Raising Global Families* (2018), Hondagneu-Sotelo's *Doméstica* (2007), and Francisco-Menchavez's *The Labor of Care* (2018), reveal that how people parent is directly shaped by the global economy; racism and xenophobia faced by those migrating to the United States for work further constrain the ways parents can raise their children.

36 M. J. Rosenfeld (2007) has argued that the nineteenth century and early twentieth century constituted an "age of independence," wherein adult children started

moving farther from home and became less financially dependent on parents, loosening parental power.

37 Silva, 2013.

38 Danziger & Ratner, 2010; Esping-Andersen, 1999.

39 Fry, 2013.

40 Fry, 2016.

41 Berlin et al., 2010; Dettling & Hsu, 2018; Maroto, 2017; Addo, 2014.

42 Cherlin & Seltzer, 2014; Hacker, 2006; Newman, 2012.

43 Zaloom, 2019.

44 A. West et al., 2017.

45 Fingerman et al., 2020

46 For, example, see Fingerman et al., 2020; Zaloom, 2019.

47 We use the term "kinship" because the parent-child tie is at the very center of our current kinship framework, and because kinship is synonymous with parents in popular culture; in our current culture, there is no kinship or family without the parent-child tie.

48 Rich, 1980.

49 I.e., the partnering of one man and one woman, including sexually, romantically, and/or residentially.

50 Heteronormativity refers to the belief that there are two and only two binary genders (men, women) and that sexual and romantic relationships are only acceptable between men and women.

51 Arnett, 2000.

52 Hess, 2000; Vangelisti, 2006.

53 Carrington, 1999.

54 Of course, some parents are deeply committed to supporting their LGBTQ kids. In Mary Robertson's *Growing Up Queer*, she shows how LGBTQ youth were surprised at their parents' levels of acceptance. And both Tey Meadow, in *Trans Kids*, and Travers, in *The Trans Generation*, focus on loving relationships between trans/GNC/GQ kids and their parents.

55 Baams et al., 2015; Cayleff, 2008; Lombardi et al., 2002; Needham & Austin, 2010; Montano et al., 2018; Powell et al., 2010; Powell, 2017; Robinson, 2018; Titlestad & Pooley, 2014; Pachankis et al., 2018; Rahilly, 2015; Solebello & Elliott, 2011; J. B. Watson, 2014; R. J. Watson et al., 2019.

56 Bouris et al., 2010; D'Amico et al., 2015; McConnell et al., 2016; Klein & Golub, 2016.

57 K. L. Acosta, 2013; Solebello & Elliott, 2011; Rahilly, 2015; Robinson, 2018; Ryan et al., 2010.

58 Rahilly, 2015.

59 McGuire, Catalpa, et al., 2016; McGuire, Kuvalanka, et al., 2016; Meadow, 2018; Rahilly, 2015; Norwood, 2013.

60 K. L. Acosta, 2010; Moore, 2011.

61 A. L. Stone, 2020.
62 Fischer & Kalmijn, 2020; Hull & Ortyl, 2019.
63 C. Reczek, 2020; Fingerman et al., 2020.
64 Merton, 1948, p. 194.

CHAPTER 2. THE RATIONALE OF LOVE AND CLOSENESS

1 In our interview, Jackie takes on the identity of trans. In our survey that was given prior to the interview, Jackie identifies "male" as her sex assigned at birth and "woman" as her gender identity.
2 Heywood, 2001; Coontz, 2006.
3 Heywood, 2001, p. 85.
4 L. Stone, 1979.
5 Heywood, 2001, p. 41, citing Badinter.
6 Bernstein, 2011.
7 Coontz, 2006; Goode, 1959; D'Emilio, 1983; J. Ward, 2020; Zelizer, 1985; L. Stone, 1979; Ariès, 1962.
8 Some scholars have suggested that in areas of high poverty, high infant mortality, and very low food security, the notion of loving one's child is a luxury. In Nancy Scheper-Hughes's remarkable book *Death Without Weeping* (1992), parents see the risk of infant death being so high that emotional attachment is not reasonable.
9 Ariès, 1962; Edin & Kefalas, 2011; Nelson, 2010.
10 Lucy is GQ/GNC and uses she/her pronouns.
11 Gilmartin, 2007.

CHAPTER 3. THE RATIONALE OF GROWTH

1 Alicia identifies as a Native American of Indigenous descent. The terminology regarding people indigenous to North America is regionally and historically specific and can include Indigenous peoples, Native American, American Indian, and First Nations; we use the language provided by our interviewees. In our interview, Alicia identifies as a trans woman; on our survey, Alicia identifies as female assigned at birth and the gender identity of a woman.
2 Gone, 2007.
3 Hain, 2016.
4 Foucault, 1980.
5 Ansara & Hegarty, 2013; Nordmarken, 2014; shuster, 2017.
6 C. Connell, 2010; Schilt, 2010.
7 Atwood, 2010; D. E. Ward, 2009.

CHAPTER 4. THE RATIONALE OF UNIQUENESS

1 Barton, 2012; Cayleff, 2008; Robinson, 2018; Titlestad & Pooley, 2014; J. B. Watson, 2014.
2 Nordqvist, 2017.

3 Natalie was assigned male at birth; their gender identity is woman, trans, and GQ/GNC.
4 A. S. Berger & Simon, 1974; Hill, 2003.
5 Taylor et al., 2013.
6 P. H. Collins, 1987; Muñoz-Laboy et al., 2009; Taylor et al., 2013.
7 P. H. Collins, 1987; Hill, 2003.
8 Zinn, 1998; Vega, 1995.
9 Randles, 2020.

PART II. HOW DO LGBTQ ADULTS ADHERE TO COMPULSORY KINSHIP?

1 Pfeffer, 2017; Reid & Golub, 2018; Stack & Burton, 1993.
2 Erickson, 1993, 2005.
3 Hochschild, 1979, 1983.
4 Erickson, 2005.
5 Di Leonardo, 1987; Pfeffer, 2017; Reid & Golub, 2018; Stack & Burton, 1993.
6 Di Leonardo, 1987.
7 Stack and Burton, 1993, p. 160.
8 Reid & Golub, 2018; Roy & Burton, 2007.
9 Erickson, 1993, 2005; Hochschild, 1983; Stack & Burton, 1993.
10 Andersen & Blosnich, 2013; Carrington, 1999; D'Amico et al., 2015; Montano et al., 2018.

CHAPTER 5. THE KIN CLOSET

1 Seidman, 2004.
2 Johnson, 2006.
3 Gill-Peterson, 2018.
4 Carter, 2004.
5 As the gay liberation movement became successful, the priorities of radical trans activists and activists of color were decentered by the needs of liberal white cis gay and lesbian people. For example, calls for abolishing the police, access to universal health care, antidiscrimination laws for trans people, and other more radical ideas were not prioritized.
6 Whether allowing gays and lesbians to serve in the military is emancipatory is up for debate given the military's colonial projects around the globe as well as the violence endemic in and resulting from the military-industrial complex. See C. Connell, forthcoming.
7 Pew Research Center, 2019a, 2019b.
8 Notably, however, the Supreme Court ruled in favor of a baker in Colorado who refused to bake a cake for a same-sex couple, creating a precedent to legally discriminate against LGBTQ people; see Beato, 2019.
9 Martos et al., 2015; Grov et al., 2006; Parks & Hughes, 2007; Norwood, 2013; Ocobock, 2013; C. Reczek, 2014.

10 Dank, 1971; Cass, 1979; R. R. Troiden, 1989; Savin-Williams & Cohen, 1996; Coleman, 1982; Hencken & O'Dowd, 1977; R. R. Troiden & Goode, 1980.
11 For critiques of the closet as a white cis concept, see Tan, 2011; Barglowski et al., 2018; Manalansan, 2003.
12 Barton, 2012; A. L. Stone, 2018; Ghaziani, 2019; B. A. Rogers, 2020; Forstie, 2020.
13 Ross, 2005.
14 Bucher, 2014; Diefendorf & Bridges, 2019.
15 Dean, 2013; R. W. Connell, 1987.
16 Kane, 2006, 2012; Meadow, 2018; Sutfin et al., 2008; L. Stacey & Padavic, 2020.
17 Jadwin-Cakmak et al., 2015; Kane, 2006; Livingston & Fourie, 2016.
18 Zimman, 2009; Brumbaugh-Johnson & Hull, 2019.
19 Kralik, 2019.
20 For an overview, see Buzuvis, 2021.
21 Simmons-Duffin, 2020; L. Acosta, 2020.
22 Cass, 1979; de Monteflores & Schultz, 1978, Orne, 2011, p. 683.
23 Orne, 2011; Langdridge, 2008; Seidman, 2004.
24 Rust, 1993; Serovich et al., 2011.
25 James et al., 2016.
26 In our interview, Jackie identifies as trans. In our survey that was given prior to the interview, Jackie signifies a male sex assigned at birth and woman as her gender identity.
27 M. M. Rogers, 2017.
28 Grady identifies as a trans woman in our interview; on our survey Grady indicated being assigned male sex at birth and having a gender identity of woman.
29 McLean, 2007.
30 McLean, 2007.
31 Cisbi women in our sample were among those who prominently used the closet as a conflict work tool.
32 Ross, 2005, p. 162.
33 It could also be that the white people we interviewed were a bit younger and therefore may be more likely to be in the closet at their current life course stage than the sample of somewhat older people of color we talked to. This may also be because our sample does not capture enough narratives of people of color to fully see the link between the closet and race. As such, we would caution strongly against saying that people of color are *not* using the closet, and refer our readers to the scholarship cited in this chapter on race and the closet.
34 Moore, 2011.

CHAPTER 6. GENDER AND SEXUALITY SCHOOL

1 Natalie was assigned male at birth and has a gender identity of woman, trans, and GQ/GNC.
2 Berk, 1985, Stacey, 2021.

3 Travers, 2019.
4 Leaper, 2002; Witt, 1997; Martin, 2009; Solebello & Elliott, 2011.
5 Sumerau & Mathers, 2019.
6 The appearance of a penis structure is the defining feature of most so-called "gender" reveals in utero. See Kane, 2012.
7 Kane, 2012.
8 Wood et al., 2002; Averett, 2016.
9 Martin, 2009; Solebello and Elliott, 2011; L. Stacey & Padavic, 2020.
10 Averett, 2016; Kane, 2006, 2012; Martin, 2005, 2009; Rahilly, 2018; L. Stacey & Padavic, 2020; C. West & Zimmerman, 1987.
11 Fields, 2001; Kane, 2006, 2012; Solebello & Elliott, 2011.
12 Lancaster, 2011.
13 shuster, 2017.
14 Robinson, 2018, 2020.
15 For an explanation of gender-neutral neo pronouns, see Tobia, 2016.
16 Zimman, 2009; James et al., 2016; Choi et al., 2015.
17 Kane, 2006, 2012; Rahilly, 2015, 2018.
18 Acosta, K. L. 2013; Moore, 2011.

CHAPTER 7. OUT OF THE CLOSET, UNDER THE RUG

1 We always did interviews with children first to get a sense of the level of their outness. Children had control over what parents knew about the study, and we had a separate recruitment website that stated the study was about parent-adult child ties, not LGBTQ parent-child ties, for children to send to their parents when they were not out. Even when children told us they were out to their parents, we never "outed" them during interviews with their parents. Instead, we would ask parents about sexuality and gender, and wait for each parent to independently tell us about their child. In the case of Carrie and a couple of other parents, we really danced around the topic, never fully saying the words.
2 Denes & Afifi, 2014.
3 Decena, 2008, 2011; also see the "glass closet," Sedgwick, 2008.
4 K. L. Acosta, 2013.
5 K. L. Acosta, 2013.
6 Decena, 2008, 2011.

CHAPTER 8. BECOMING NORMAL

1 Duggan, 2002; D. Rosenfeld, 2009.
2 Warner, 2000.
3 Stryker, 2008, pp. 147–148.
4 Brainer, 2019, p. 89. Also see Duggan, 2002; Warner, 2000; Sumerau et al., 2020.
5 Ward, 2020. Also see Pascoe, 2009.

6 K. L. Acosta, 2010; Han, 2015; Bérubé, 2001; Warner, 2000.
7 Duggan, 2002.
8 J. Ward, 2020.
9 Ocobock, 2013.
10 Suggesting that disabled people are not to be celebrated and that a nonheterosexual sexuality is a disability is both ableist and homophobic.
11 Max is a trans, genderqueer, gender-nonconforming person who was assigned female at birth.
12 shuster, 2017; Schilt & Westbrook, 2009.
13 A. L. Stone, 2020, p. 1117.
14 Fetner & Heath, 2016; Ocobock, 2013.
15 K. L. Acosta, 2008, 2010; Ecklund, 2005; García et al., 2008; Hom, 1994; Li & Orleans, 2001; Loughrin, 2015; Ocampo, 2014; Ocampo & Soodjinda, 2016; Tuthill, 2016; Yip, 1997.
16 Hunter, 2010.

CHAPTER 9. OUT OF THE FAMILY

1 Blake, 2017, p. 532.
2 Gilligan et al., 2015; Conti, 2015; Pillemer, 2020.
3 Conti, 2015.
4 Agllias, 2011, 2013, 2015; Gilligan et al., 2015.
5 Scharp et al., 2015; Dorrance Hall, 2017.
6 Agllias, 2016; Cayleff, 2008; Scharp & Dorrance Hall, 2017; Scharp & McLaren, 2018; Weston, 1997; J. B. Watson, 2014.
7 Stone, Nimmons, & Davis, 2019; also see Cayleff, 2008; Robinson, 2018, 2020; Titlestad & Pooley, 2014; J. B. Watson, 2014; Barton, 2012.
8 Scharp & Dorrance Hall, 2017, p. 28.
9 Conti, 2015.
10 Brad identifies in our interview both as a man and as trans; on our survey he identified as a man who was assigned female at birth.
11 Taylor et al., 2013.
12 Stone et al., 2019.
13 Gerstel, 2011.

CONCLUSION

1 Hull & Ortyl, 2019.
2 The original quote reads, "In the absence of choice, women will remain dependent on the chance or luck of particular relationships and will have no collective power to determine the meaning and place of sexuality in their lives." Rich, 1980, p. 659.
3 For example, Carrington, 1999; Chatters, et al., 1994; Choi et al., 2015; Collins, P.H., 2004; Decena, 2011; Francisco-Menchavez, 2018; Furstenberg et al., 2020;

Gerstel, 2011; Hunter, 2010; Hondagheu-Sotelo, 2007; Ingraham, 1994; Robinson, 2020; Pfeffer, 2017; Taylor et al., 2013.

4 Levitsky, 2014.

5 Zaloom, 2019, among many others we have cited throughout this book (see Chapter 1 especially).

6 C. Collins, 2019; Kaufman, 2020.

7 Zaloom, 2019.

8 We also think that reducing the linkages between parents and children's finances would reduce inequality more broadly. Intergenerational wealth transfer is a massive driver of economic inequality in the United States. Adults with wealthy parents expect that parents will pass on their wealth—in the form of houses, down payments, trust funds, and the like. This means that only the lucky few kids who have wealthy or stably middle-class parents can afford to really "make it" in adulthood.

9 Abrego, 2014.

10 Taylor et al., 2013.

11 Nelson, 2020.

12 Allen et al., 2011; J. Stacey, 1998; DePaulo, 2015; Dewaele et al., 2011.

13 Also see Hull & Ortyl, 2019.

14 Weston 1997; Weeks et al., 2001; Hull & Ortyl, 2019.

15 Chatters et al., 1994, p. 303.

16 Nelson, 2006.

17 Meadow, 2018; Travers, 2019; Rahilly, 2015.

METHODOLOGICAL APPENDIX

1 A. L. Stone, 2018; Herring, 2010.

2 Hasenbush et al., 2014.

3 A. L. Stone, 2018; Brown-Saracino & Parker, 2017.

4 Yu, 2010.

5 Both interview guides were written as a set of questions that should be flexible and interpreted uniquely in each interview. All questions were followed up to gain qualitative stories and assessments even when this is not apparent in the guide. Follow-up questions included: How did that make you feel? Hypothetical (what would happen if that did occur)? What do you mean by that? Can you give me an example? What do you think your parents/family member thought about that? What is your ideal relationship/event/experience? What would you like to have happen?

REFERENCES

Abrego, L. J. 2014. *Sacrificing families: Navigating laws, labor, and love across borders.* Stanford University Press.

Acosta, K. L. 2008. Lesbianas in the borderlands: Shifting identities and imagined communities. *Gender and Society, 22*(5), 639–659.

Acosta, K. L. 2010. "How could you do this to me?": How lesbian, bisexual, and queer Latinas negotiate sexual identity with their families. *Black Women, Gender and Families, 4*(1), 63–85.

Acosta, K. L. 2013. *Amigas y amantes: Sexually nonconforming Latinas negotiate family.* Rutgers University Press.

Acosta, L. 2020. The real list of Trump's "unprecedented steps" for the LGBTQ community. Human Rights Campaign. https://www.hrc.org

Addo, F. R. 2014. Debt, cohabitation, and marriage in young adulthood. *Demography, 51*(5), 1677–1701.

Agllias, K. 2011. No longer on speaking terms: The losses associated with family estrangement at the end of life. *Families in Society, 92*(1), 107–113.

Agllias, K. 2013. The gendered experience of family estrangement in later life. *Affilia, 28*(3), 309–321.

Agllias, K. 2015. Difference, choice, and punishment: Parental beliefs and understandings about adult child estrangement. *Australian Social Work, 68*(1), 115–129.

Agllias, K. 2016. Disconnection and decision-making: Adult children explain their reasons for estranging from parents. *Australian Social Work, 69*(1), 92–104.

Ahmed, S. 2010. The promise of happiness. Duke University Press.

Allen, K. R., Blieszner, R., & Roberto, K. A. 2011. Perspectives on extended family and fictive kin in the later years: Strategies and meanings of kin reinterpretation. *Journal of Family Issues, 32*(9), 1156–1177.

Andersen, J. P., & Blosnich, J. 2013. Disparities in adverse childhood experiences among sexual minority and heterosexual adults: Results from a multi-state probability-based sample. *PLOS ONE, 8*(1), e54691.

Ansara, Y. G., & Hegarty, P. 2013. Misgendering in English language contexts: Applying non-cisgenderist methods to feminist research. *International Journal of Multiple Research Approaches, 7*(2), 160–177.

Ariès, P. 1962. *Centuries of childhood.* Penguin.

Arnett, J. J. 2000. Emerging adulthood: A theory of development from the late teens through the twenties. *American Psychologist, 55*(5), 469.

Atwood, B. A. 2010. *Adoption and custody conflicts over American Indian children.* Carolina Academic Press.

Averett, K. H. 2016. The gender buffet: LGBTQ parents resisting heteronormativity. *Gender and Society*, *30*(2), 189–212.

Baams, L., Grossman, A. H., & Russell, S. T. 2015. Minority stress and mechanisms of risk for depression and suicidal ideation among lesbian, gay, and bisexual youth. *Developmental Psychology*, *51*(5), 688–696.

Barglowski, K., Amelina, A., & Bilecen, B. 2018. Coming out within transnational families: intimate confessions under Western eyes. *Social Identities*, *24*(6), 836–851.

Barton, B. 2012. *Pray the gay away: The extraordinary lives of Bible Belt gays*. NYU Press.

Baxter, L. A., Henauw, C., Huisman, D., Livesay, C., Norwood, K., Su, H., & Young, B. 2009. Lay conceptions of "family": A replication and extension. *Journal of Family Communication*, 9, 170–189.

Beato, M. 2019. Let them eat cake or let him not bake: Summary and analysis of *Masterpiece Cakeshop v. Colorado Civil Rights Commission. Florida Law Review, 71*, 1347–1362.

Berger, A. S., & Simon, W. 1974. Black families and the Moynihan Report: A research evaluation. *Social Problems*, *22*(2), 145–161.

Berger, P. L., & Luckmann, T. 1966. *The social construction of reality: A treatise in the sociology of knowledge*. Anchor.

Berk, S. F. 1985. *The gender factory: The appointment of work in American households.* Plenum Press.

Berlant, L. 2011. *Cruel optimism*. Duke University Press.

Berlin, G., Furstenberg, F., & Waters, M. C. 2010. The transition to adulthood: Introducing the issue. *The Future of Children*, *20*(1), 3–18.

Bernstein, R. 2011. *Racial innocence: Performing American childhood and race from slavery to civil rights*. NYU Press.

Bérubé, A. 2001. "How gay stays white and what kind of white it stays." In B. B. Rasmussen, E. Klinenberg, I. J. Nexica, & M. Wray (Eds.), *The making and unmaking of whiteness* (pp. 234–265). Duke University Press.

Blake, L. 2017. Parents and children who are estranged in adulthood: A review and discussion of the literature. *Journal of Family Theory and Review* 9(4): 521–36.

Bosley-Smith, E., & Reczek, R. Forthcoming. "Why LGBTQ adults keep ambivalent ties with parents: Theorizing 'solidarity rationales.' *Social Problems.*

Bouris, A., Guilamo-Ramos, V., Pickard, A., Shiu, C., Loosier, P. S., Dittus, P., Gloppen, K., & Waldmiller, J. M. 2010. A systematic review of parental influences on the health and well-being of lesbian, gay, and bisexual youth: Time for a new public health research and practice agenda. *Journal of Primary Prevention*, *31*(5–6), 273–309.

Brainer, A. 2019. *Queer kinship and family change in Taiwan*. Rutgers University Press.

Brown-Saracino, J., & Parker, J. N. 2017. "What is up with my sisters? Where are you?": The origins and consequences of lesbian-friendly place reputations for LBQ migrants." *Sexualities*, *20*(7), 835–874.

Brumbaugh-Johnson, S. M., & Hull, K. E. 2019. Coming out as transgender: Navigating the social implications of a transgender identity. *Journal of Homosexuality, 66*(8), 1148–1177.

Bucher, J. 2014. But he can't be gay": The relationship between masculinity and homophobia in father-son relationships. *Journal of Men's Studies, 22*(3), 222–237.

Bulanda, J. R. 2011. Doing family, doing gender, doing religion: Structured ambivalence and the religion-family connection. *Journal of Family Theory and Review, 3*(3), 179–197.

Buzuvis, E., 2021. Law, policy, and the participation of transgender athletes in the United States. *Sport Management Review*, 24(3), 439–451.

Carrington, C. 1999. *No place like home: Relationships and family life among lesbians and gay men*. University of Chicago Press.

Carter, D. 2004. *Stonewall: The riots that sparked the gay revolution*. Macmillan.

Cass, V. C. 1979. Homosexual identity formation: A theoretical model. *Journal of homosexuality*, 4(3), 219–235.

Cayleff, S. 2008. Feeding the hand that bit you: Lesbian daughters at mid-life negotiating parental caretaking. *Journal of Lesbian Studies, 12*(2–3), 237–254.

Chatters, L. M., Taylor, R. J., & Jayakody, R. 1994. Fictive kinship relations in black extended families. *Journal of Comparative Family Studies*, 25(3), 297–312.

Cherlin, A. 1978. Remarriage as an incomplete institution. *American Journal of Sociology, 84*(3), 634–650.

Cherlin, A. J., & Seltzer, J. A. 2014. Family complexity, the family safety net, and public policy. *ANNALS of the American Academy of Political and Social Science, 654*(1), 231–239.

Choi, S. K., Wilson, B. D., Shelton, J., & Gates, G. J. 2015. Serving our youth 2015: The needs and experiences of lesbian, gay, bisexual, transgender, and questioning youth experiencing homelessness. Williams Institute. https://escholarship.org

Coleman, E. 1982. Developmental stages of the coming out process. *Journal of Homosexuality, 7*(2–3), 31–43.

Collins, C. 2019. *Making motherhood work*. Princeton.

Collins, P. H. 1986. Learning from the outsider within: The sociological significance of Black feminist thought. *Social Problems, 33*(6), s14–s32.

Collins, P. H. 1987. The meaning of motherhood in Black culture and Black mother-daughter relationships. *Sage, 4*(2), 3.

Collins, P. H. 1999. Reflections on the outsider within. *Journal of Career Development, 26*(1), 85–88.

Collins, P. H. 2004. *Black sexual politics: African Americans, gender, and the new racism*. Routledge.

Connell, C. 2010. Doing, undoing, or redoing gender? Learning from the workplace experiences of transpeople" *Gender and Society, 24*(1), 31–55.

Connell, C. Forthcoming. *A few good gays: The homonormative bargain behind the US military's policy transformation*. University of California Press.

Connell, R. W. 1987. *Gender and power*. Stanford University Press.

Conti, R. P. 2015. Family estrangement: Establishing a prevalence rate. *Journal of Psychology and Behavioral Science, 3*(2), 28–35.

Coontz, S. 2006. *Marriage, a history: How love conquered marriage*. Penguin.

D'Amico, E., Julien, D., Tremblay, N., & Chartrand, E. 2015. Gay, lesbian, and bisexual youths coming out to their parents: Parental reactions and youths' outcomes. *Journal of GLBT Family Studies, 11*(5), 411–437.

Dank, B. M. 1971. Coming out in the gay world. *Psychiatry, 34*(2), 180–197.

Danziger, S., & Ratner, D. 2010. Labor market outcomes and the transition to adulthood. *The Future of Children*, 20(1), 133–158.

Davis, G. 2015. *Contesting intersex: The dubious diagnosis*. NYU Press.

Dean, J. J. 2013. Heterosexual masculinities, anti-homophobias, and shifts in hegemonic masculinity: The identity practices of black and white heterosexual men. *Sociological Quarterly, 54*(4), 534–560.

Decena, C. U. 2008. Tacit subjects. *GLQ: A Journal of Lesbian and Gay Studies, 14*(2–3), 339–359.

Decena, C. U. 2011. *Tacit subjects: Belonging and same-sex desire among Dominican immigrant men*. Duke University Press.

D'Emilio, J. 1983. Capitalism and gay identity. In K. V. Hansen & A. I. Garey (Eds.), *Families in the US: Kinship and domestic politics* (pp. 131–41). Temple University Press.

De Monteflores, C., & Schultz, S. J. 1978. Coming out: Similarities and differences for lesbians and gay men. *Journal of Social Issues, 34*(3), 59–72.

Denes, A., & Afifi, T. D. 2014. Coming out again: Exploring GLBQ individuals' communication with their parents after the first coming out. *Journal of GLBT Family Studies, 10*(3), 298–325.

DePaulo, B. 2015. *How we live now: Redefining home and family in the 21st century*. Simon and Schuster.

Dettling, L. J., & Hsu, J. W. 2018. Returning to the nest: Debt and parental co-residence among young adults. *Labour Economics*, 54, 225–236.

Dewaele, A., Cox, N., Van den Berghe, W., & Vincke, J. 2011. Families of choice? Exploring the supportive networks of lesbians, gay men, and bisexuals. *Journal of Applied Social Psychology, 41*(2), 312–331.

Diefendorf, S., & Bridges, T. 2019. On the enduring relationship between masculinity and homophobia. *Sexualities*, 1363460719876843.

Di Leonardo, M. 1987. The female world of cards and holidays. *Signs, 12*, 440–453.

Doepke, M., & Zilibotti, F. 2019. *Love, money, and parenting: How economics explains the way we raise our kids*. Princeton University Press.

Dorrance Hall, E. 2017. The process of family member marginalization: Turning points experienced by "black sheep." *Personal Relationships, 24*(3), 491–512.

Dow, D. M. 2019. *Mothering while Black: Boundaries and burdens of middle-class parenthood*. University of California Press.

Duggan, L. 2002. The new homonormativity: The sexual politics of neoliberalism. *Materializing democracy: Toward a revitalized cultural politics, 10*, 9780822383901-007.

Ecklund, E. H. 2005. Different identity accounts for Catholic women. *Review of Religious Research, 47*, 135–49.

Edin, K., & Kefalas, M. 2011. *Promises I can keep: Why poor women put motherhood before marriage*. University of California Press.

Erickson, R. J. 1993. Reconceptualizing family work: The effect of emotion work on perceptions of marital quality. *Journal of Marriage and Family*, 54(4), 888–900.

Erickson, R. J. 2005. Why emotion work matters: Sex, gender, and the division of household labor. *Journal of Marriage and Family, 67*(2), 337–351.

Esping-Andersen, G. 1999. *Social foundations of postindustrial economies*. Oxford University Press.

Fenstermaker, S., & West, C. (Eds.). 2002. *Doing gender, doing difference: Inequality, power, and institutional change*. Psychology Press.

Fetner, T., & Heath, M. 2016. Editor's Pick: Do same-sex and straight weddings aspire to the fairytale? Women's conformity and resistance to traditional weddings. *Sociological Perspectives, 59*(4), 721–742.

Fields, J. 2001. Normal queers: Straight parents respond to their children's "coming out." *Symbolic Interaction*, 24(2), 165–167.

Fingerman, K. L., Cheng, Y. P., Wesselmann, E. D., Zarit, S., Furstenberg, F., & Birditt, K. S. 2012. Helicopter parents and landing pad kids: Intense parental support of grown children. *Journal of Marriage and Family, 74*(4), 880–896.

Fingerman, K. L., Huo, M., & Birditt, K. S. 2020. A decade of research on intergenerational ties: Technological, economic, political, and demographic changes. *Journal of Marriage and Family, 82*(1), 383–403.

Fischer, M. M., & Kalmijn, M. 2020. Do adult men and women in same-sex relationships have weaker ties to their parents? *Journal of Family Psychology, 35*(3), 288–298.

Forstie, C. 2020. Theory making from the middle: Researching LGBTQ communities in small cities. *City and Community, 19*(1), 153–168.

Foucault, M. 1980. *The history of sexuality. Volume I: An Introduction* (R. Hurley, Trans.). Vintage.

Francisco-Menchavez, V. 2018. *The labor of care: Filipina migrants and transnational families in the digital age*. University of Illinois Press.

Fry, R. 2013. A rising share of young adults live in their parents' home. Pew Research Center. https://www.pewsocialtrends.org

Fry, R. 2016. For the first time in modern era, living with parents edges out other living arrangements for 18- to 34-year-olds. Pew Research Center. https://assets.pewresearch.org

Fry, R., Passel, J., & Cohn, D. 2020. A majority of young adults in the U.S. live with their parents for the first time since the Great Depression. Pew Research Center. https://www.pewresearch.org

Furstenberg, F. F., Harris, L. E., Pesando, L. M., & Reed, M. N. 2020. Kinship practices among alternative family forms in Western industrialized societies. *Journal of Marriage and Family, 82*(5), 1403–1430.

Gallagher, S. K. 2003. *Evangelical identity and gendered family life*. Rutgers University Press.

Gallagher, S. K. 2007. Agency, resources, and identity: Lower-income women's experiences in Damascus. *Gender and Society, 21(2)*, 227–249.

García, D. I., Gray-Stanley, J., & Ramirez-Valles, J. 2008. "The priest obviously doesn't know that I'm gay": The religious and spiritual journeys of Latino gay men. *Journal of Homosexuality, 55*(3), 411–436.

Gerstel, N. 2011. Rethinking families and community: The color, class, and centrality of extended kin ties. *Sociological Forum, 26*(1), 1–20.

Gerth, H. H., & Mills, C. W. 1953. *Character and social structure*. Harcourt, Brace.

Ghaziani, A. 2019. Cultural archipelagos: New directions in the study of sexuality and space. *City and Community, 18*(1), 4–22.

Gill-Hopple, K., & Brage-Hudson, D. (2012). Compadrazgo: A literature review. *Journal of Transcultural Nursing, 23*(2), 117–123.

Gill-Peterson, J. 2018. *Histories of the transgender child*. University of Minnesota Press.

Gilligan, M., Suitor, J. J., & Pillemer, K. 2015. Estrangement between mothers and adult children: The role of norms and values. *Journal of Marriage and Family, 77*(4), 908–920.

Gilmartin, S. K. 2007. Crafting heterosexual masculine identities on campus: College men talk about romantic love. *Men and Masculinities,* 9(4), 530–539.

Goff, P. A., Jackson, M. C., Di Leone, B. A. L., Culotta, C. M., & DiTomasso, N. A. 2014. The essence of innocence: Consequences of dehumanizing Black children. *Journal of Personality and Social Psychology, 106*(4), 526–545.

Gollaher, D. L. 2001. *Circumcision: A history of the world's most controversial surgery*. Basic Books.

Gone, J. P. 2007. "We never was happy living like a Whiteman": Mental health disparities and the postcolonial predicament in American Indian communities. *American Journal of Community Psychology*, 40(3–4), 290–300.

Goode, W. J. 1959. The theoretical importance of love. *American Sociological Review*, 24(1), 38–47.

Grov, C., Bimbi, D. S., Nanín, J. E., & Parsons, J. T. 2006. Race, ethnicity, gender, and generational factors associated with the coming-out process among gay, lesbian, and bisexual individuals. *Journal of Sex Research*, 43(2), 115–121.

Hacker, J. S. 2006. *The great risk shift: The assault on American jobs, families: Health care, and retirement and how you can fight back*. Oxford University Press.

Hain, M. 2016. We are here for you: The It Gets Better Project, queering rural space, and cultivating queer media literacy. In M. L. Gray, C. R. Johnson, & B. J. Gilley (Eds.), *Queering the countryside: New frontiers in rural queer studies* (pp. 159–180). NYU Press.

Han, C. W. 2015. *Geisha of a different kind: Race and sexuality in gaysian America.* NYU Press.

Hartnett, C. S., Fingerman, K. L., & Birditt, K. S. 2018. Without the ties that bind: US young adults who lack active parental relationships. *Advances in Life Course Research, 35*, 103–113.

Hasenbush, A., Flores, A., Kastanis, A., Sears, B., & Gates, G. 2014. The LGBT divide: A data portrait of LGBT people in the Midwestern, Mountain and Southern states. Williams Institute.

Hays, S. 1998. *The cultural contradictions of motherhood.* Yale University Press.

Hencken, J. D., & O'Dowd, W. T. 1977. Coming out as an aspect of identity formation. *Gai Saber, 1*(1), 18–22.

Herring, S. 2010. *Another country: Queer anti-urbanism.* NYU Press.

Hess, J. A. 2000. Maintaining nonvoluntary relationships with disliked partners: An investigation into the use of distancing behaviors. *Human Communication Research, 26*(3), 458–488.

Heywood, C. 2001. *A history of childhood: Children and childhood in the West from medieval to modern times.* Polity Press.

Hill, R. B. 2003. *The strengths of Black families.* University Press of America.

Hochschild, A. 1979. Emotion work, feeling roles, and social structure. *American Journal of Sociology, 85*, 551–575.

Hochschild, A. 1983. *The managed heart: Commercialization of human feeling.* University of California Press.

Hochschild, A., & Machung, A. 2012. *The second shift: Working families and the revolution at home.* Penguin.

Hom, Alice Y. 1994. Stories from the homefront: Perspectives of Asian American parents with lesbian daughters and gay sons. *Amerasia Journal, 20*(1), 19–32.

Hondagneu-Sotelo, P. 2007. *Doméstica: Immigrant workers cleaning and caring in the shadows of affluence, with a new preface.* University of California Press.

Hull, K. E., & Ortyl, T. A. 2019. Conventional and cutting-edge: Definitions of family in LGBT communities. *Sexuality Research and Social Policy, 16*(1), 31–43.

Hunter, M. A. 2010. All the gays are White and all the Blacks are straight: Black gay men, identity, and community. *Sexuality Research and Social Policy, 7*(2), 81–92.

Ingraham, C. 1994. The heterosexual imaginary: Feminist sociology and theories of gender. *Sociological Theory*, 12(2), 203–219.

Jadwin-Cakmak, L. A., Pingel, E. S., Harper, G. W., & Bauermeister, J. A. 2015. Coming out to dad: Young gay and bisexual men's experiences disclosing same-sex attraction to their fathers. *American Journal of Men's Health, 9*(4), 274–288.

James, S., Herman, J., Rankin, S., Keisling, M., Mottet, L., & Anafi, M. A. 2016. *The report of the 2015 U.S. Transgender Survey.* National Center for Transgender Equality.

Johnson, D. K. 2006. *The lavender scare: The Cold War persecution of gays and lesbians.* University of Chicago Press.

Kane, E. W. 2006. "No way my boys are going to be like that!": Parents' responses to children's gender nonconformity. *Gender and Society*, *20*(2), 149–176.

Kane, E. W. 2012. *The gender trap: Parents and the pitfalls of raising boys and girls*. NYU Press.

Kaufman, G. 2020. *Fixing parental leave*. NYU Press.

Klein, A., & Golub, S. A. 2016. Family rejection as a predictor of suicide attempts and substance misuse among transgender and gender nonconforming adults. *LGBT Health*, *3*(3), 193–199.

Kralik, J. 2019. "Bathroom Bill" legislative tracking: 2017 State legislation. National Conference of State Legislatures. https://www.ncsl.org

Lan, P. C. 2018. *Raising global families: Parenting, immigration, and class in Taiwan and the US*. Stanford University Press.

Lancaster, R. N. 2011. *Sex panic and the punitive state*. University of California Press.

Langdridge, D. 2008. Are you angry or are you heterosexual? A queer critique of lesbian and gay models of identity development. In L. Moon (Ed.), *Feeling queer or queer feelings? Radical approaches to counselling sex, sexualities and genders* (pp. 23–35). Routledge/Taylor and Francis Group.

Lareau, A. 2011. *Unequal childhoods: Class, race, and family life*. University of California Press.

Leaper, C. 2002. Parenting boys and girls. In M. H. Bornstein (Ed.), *Handbook of parenting* (vol. 1, pp. 189–225). Lawrence Earlbaum.

Levitsky, S. R. 2014. *Caring for our own: Why there is no political demand for new American social welfare rights*. Oxford University Press.

Li, L., & Orleans, M. 2001. Coming out discourses of Asian American lesbians. *Sexuality and Culture*, *5*(2), 57–78.

Livingston, J., & Fourie, E. 2016. The experiences and meanings that shape heterosexual fathers' relationships with their gay sons in South Africa. *Journal of Homosexuality*, *63*(12), 1630–1659.

Lombardi, E. L., Wilchins, R. A., Priesing, D., & Malouf, D. 2002. Gender violence: Transgender experiences with violence and discrimination. *Journal of Homosexuality*, *42*(1), 89–101.

Lopez, R. A. 1999. Las comadres as a social support system. *Affilia*, *14*(1), 24–41.

Loughrin, S. M. 2015. Queer Chicano families: The importance of converging literature on queer families, Chicano families, and Chicano queers. *Sociology Compass*, *9*(3), 224–234.

Lowrey, S., & Shepard, J. P. 2010. *Kicked out*. Homofactus Press.

Manalansan, M. F., IV. 2003. *Global divas: Filipino gay men in the diaspora*. Duke University Press.

Maroto, M. 2017. When the kids live at home: Coresidence, parental assets, and economic insecurity. *Journal of Marriage and Family*, *79*(4), 1041–1059.

Martin, K. A. 2005. William wants a doll. Can he have one? Feminists, child care advisors, and gender-neutral child rearing. *Gender and Society*, *19*(4), 456–479.

Martin, K. A. 2009. Normalizing heterosexuality: Mothers' assumptions, talk, and strategies with young children. *American Sociological Review, 74*(2), 190–207.

Martos, A. J., Nezhad, S., & Meyer, I. H. 2015. Variations in sexual identity milestones among lesbians, gay men, and bisexuals. *Sexuality Research and Social Policy, 12*(1), 24–33.

McConnell, E. A., Birkett, M., & Mustanski, B. 2016. Families matter: Social support and mental health trajectories among lesbian, gay, bisexual, and transgender youth. *Journal of Adolescent Health, 59*(6), 674–680.

McGuire, J. K., Catalpa, J. M., Lacey, V., & Kuvalanka, K. A. 2016. Ambiguous loss as a framework for interpreting gender transitions in families. *Journal of Family Theory and Review, 8*(3), 373–385.

McGuire, J. K., Kuvalanka, K. A., Catalpa, J. M., & Toomey, R. B. 2016. Transfamily theory: How the presence of trans* family members informs gender development in families. *Journal of Family Theory and Review, 8*(1), 60–73.

McLanahan, S., & Jacobsen, W. 2015. Diverging destinies revisited. In P. R. Amato, A. Booth, S. M. McHale, & J. Van Hook (Eds.), *Families in an era of increasing inequality* (pp. 3–23). Springer Cham.

McLean, K. 2007. Hiding in the closet? Bisexuals, coming out and the disclosure imperative. *Journal of Sociology, 43*(2), 151–166.

Meadow, T. 2018. *Trans kids: Being gendered in the twenty-first century*. University of California Press.

Merton, R. K. 1948. The self-fulfilling prophecy. *Antioch Review, 8*(2), 193–210.

Mitchell, M. N. 2008. *Raising freedom's child: Black children and visions of the future after slavery*. NYU Press.

Montano, G. T., Thoma, B. C., Paglisotti, T., Weiss, P. M., Shultz, M. K., McCauley, H. L., Miller, E., & Marshal, M. P. 2018. Disparities in parental support and parental attachment between heterosexual and sexual minority youth: A meta-analysis. *Journal of Adolescent Health, 62*(2), S32–S33.

Moore, M. 2011. *Invisible families: Gay identities, relationships, and motherhood among Black women*. University of California Press.

Morgan, D. 2002. *Making men into fathers: Men, masculinities and the social politics of fatherhood*. Cambridge University Press.

Muñoz-Laboy, M., Leau, C. J. Y., Sriram, V., Weinstein, H. J., del Aquila, E. V., & Parker, R. 2009. Bisexual desire and familism: Latino/a bisexual young men and women in New York City. *Culture, Health and Sexuality, 11*(3), 331–344.

Naples, N. 2001. A member of the funeral: An introspective ethnography. In M. Bernstein & R. Reimann (Eds.), *Queer families, queer politics* (pp. 21–43). Columbia University Press.

Needham, B. L., & Austin, E. L. 2010. Sexual orientation, parental support, and health during the transition to young adulthood. *Journal of Youth and Adolescence, 39*(10), 1189–1198.

Nelson, M. K. 2006. Single mothers "do" family. *Journal of Marriage and Family*, *68*(4), 781–795.

Nelson, M. K. 2010. *Parenting out of control: Anxious parents in uncertain times*. NYU Press.

Nelson, M. K. 2020. *Like family: Narratives of fictive kinship*. Rutgers University Press.

Newman, K. S. 2012. *The accordion family: Boomerang kids, anxious parents, and the private toll of global competition*. Beacon Press.

Nordmarken, S. 2014. Becoming ever more monstrous: Feeling transgender in-betweenness. *Qualitative Inquiry*, *20*(1), 37–50.

Nordqvist, P. 2017. Genetic thinking and everyday living: On family practices and family imaginaries. *Sociological Review*, *65*(4), 865–881.

Norwood, K. 2013. Grieving gender: Trans-identities, transition, and ambiguous loss. *Communication Monographs*, *80*(1), 24–45.

Ocampo, A. C. 2014. The gay second generation: Sexual identity and family relations of Filipino and Latino gay men. *Journal of Ethnic and Migration Studies*, *40*(1), 155–173.

Ocampo, A. C., & Soodjinda, D. 2016. Invisible Asian Americans: The intersection of sexuality, race, and education among gay Asian Americans. *Race Ethnicity and Education*, *19*(3), 480–499.

Ocobock, A. 2013. The power and limits of marriage: Married gay men's family relationships. *Journal of Marriage and Family*, *75*(1), 191–205.

Offer, S., & Fischer, C. S. 2018. Difficult people: Who is perceived to be demanding in personal networks and why are they there? *American Sociological Review*, *83*(1), 111–142.

Onwuachi-Willig, A. 2017. Policing the boundaries of whiteness: The tragedy of being out of place from Emmett Till to Trayvon Martin. *Iowa Law Review, 102(3)*, 1113–1185.

Orne, J. 2011. "You will always have to 'out' yourself": Reconsidering coming out through strategic outness. *Sexualities*, *14*(6), 681–703.

Pachankis, J. E., Sullivan, T. J., & Moore, N. F. 2018. A 7-year longitudinal study of sexual minority young men's parental relationships and mental health. *Journal of Family Psychology*, *32*(8), 1068–1077.

Parks, C. A., & Hughes, T. L. 2007. Age differences in lesbian identity development and drinking. *Substance Use and Misuse*, *42*(2–3), 361–380.

Pascoe, P. 2009. *What comes naturally: Miscegenation law and the making of race in America*. Oxford University Press on Demand.

Pew Research Center. 2019a. 5 facts about same sex marriage [Fact Tank]. https://www.pewresearch.org

Pew Research Center. 2019b. Majority of public favors same-sex marriage, but divisions persist [Fact Tank]. https://www.people-press.org

Pfeffer, C. A. 2017. *Queering families: The postmodern partnerships of cisgender women and transgender men*. Oxford University Press.

Pillemer, K. 2020. *Fault line: Fractured families and how to mend them*. Avery.

Pillemer, K., Suitor, J. J., Mock, S. E., Sabir, M., Pardo, T. B., & Sechrist, J. 2007. Capturing the complexity of intergenerational relations: Exploring ambivalence within later-life families. *Journal of Social Issues*, *63*(4), 775–791.

Powell, B. 2017. Changing counts, counting change: Toward a more inclusive definition of family. *Journal of the Indiana Academy of the Social Sciences*, *17*(1), 2.

Powell, B., Blozendahl, C., Geist, C., & Steelman, L. C. 2010. *Counted out: Same-sex relations and Americans' definitions of family*. Russell Sage Foundation.

Rahilly, E. P. 2015. The gender binary meets the gender-variant child: Parents' negotiations with childhood gender variance. *Gender and Society*, *29*(3), 338–361.

Rahilly, E. P. 2018. Re-interpreting gender and sexuality: Parents of gender-nonconforming children. *Sexuality and Culture*, *22*(4), 1391–1411.

Randles, J. M. 2020. *Essential dads: The inequality and politics of fathering*. University of California Press.

Reardon, S. F., & Owens, A. 2014. 60 years after *Brown*: Trends and consequences of school segregation. *Annual Review of Sociology, 40, 199–218.*

Reczek, C. 2014. The intergenerational relationships of gay men and lesbian women. *Journals of Gerontology Series B: Psychological Sciences and Social Sciences*, *69*(6), 909–919.

Reczek, C. 2020. Sexual- and gender-minority families: A 2010 to 2020 decade in review. *Journal of Marriage and Family*, *82*(1), 300–325.

Reczek, R., & Bosley-Smith, E. 2021. How LGBTQ adults maintain ties with rejecting parents: Theorizing "conflict work" as family work. *Journal of Marriage and Family*, *83*(4), 1134–1153.

Reid, M., & Golub, A. 2018. Low-income Black men's kin work: Social fatherhood in cohabiting stepfamilies. *Journal of Family Issues*, *39*(4), 960–984.

Rich, A. 1980. Compulsory heterosexuality and lesbian existence. *Signs: Journal of Women in Culture and Society*, *5*(4), 631–660.

Roberts, D. 2009. *Shattered bonds: The color of child welfare*. Civitas Books.

Robertson, M. 2018. *Growing up queer: Kids and the remaking of LGBTQ identity*. NYU Press.

Robinson, B. A. 2018. Conditional families and lesbian, gay, bisexual, transgender, and queer youth homelessness: Gender, sexuality, family instability, and rejection. *Journal of Marriage and Family*, *80*(2), 383–396.

Robinson, B. A. 2020. *Coming out to the streets: LGBTQ youth experiencing homelessness*. University of California Press.

Rogers, B. A. 2020. *Trans men in the south: Becoming men*. Lexington Books.

Rogers, M. M. 2017. The intersection of cisgenderism and hate crime: Learning from trans people's narratives. *Journal of Family Strengths*, *17*(2), article 5.

Rosenfeld, D. 2009. Heteronormativity and homonormativity as practical and moral resources: The case of lesbian and gay elders. *Gender and Society*, *23*(5), 617–638.

Rosenfeld, M. J. 2007. *The age of independence: Interracial unions, same-sex unions, and the changing American family*. Harvard University Press.

Ross, M. B. 2005. Beyond the closet as raceless paradigm. In E. P. Johnson & M. G. Henderson (Eds.), *Black queer studies: A critical anthology* (pp. 161–189). Duke University Press.

Roy, K., & Burton, L. 2007. Mothering through recruitment: Kinscription of nonresidential fathers and father figures in low-income families. *Family Relations*, 56(1), 24–39.

Rust, P. C. 1993. "Coming out" in the age of social constructionism: Sexual identity formation among lesbian and bisexual women. *Gender and Society*, *7*(1), 50–77.

Ryan, C., Russell, S. T., Huebner, D., Diaz, R., & Sanchez, J. 2010. Family acceptance in adolescence and the health of LGBT young adults. *Journal of Child and Adolescent Psychiatric Nursing*, *23*(4), 205–213.

Sarkisian, N. 2006. "Doing family ambivalence": Nuclear and extended families in single mothers' lives. *Journal of Marriage and Family*, *68*(4), 804–811.

Savin-Williams, R. C., & Cohen, K. M. 1996. *The lives of lesbians, gays, and bisexuals: Children to adults*. Harcourt Brace College Publishers.

Scharp, K. M., & Dorrance Hall, E. 2017. Family marginalization, alienation, and estrangement: Questioning the nonvoluntary status of family relationships. *Annals of the International Communication Association*, *41*(1), 28–45.

Scharp, K. M., & McLaren, R. M. 2018. Uncertainty issues and management in adult children's stories of their estrangement with their parents. *Journal of Social and Personal Relationships*, *35*(6), 811–830.

Scharp, K. M., Thomas, L. J., & Paxman, C. G. 2015. "It was the straw that broke the camel's back": Exploring the distancing processes communicatively constructed in parent-child estrangement backstories. *Journal of Family Communication*, *15*(4), 330–348.

Scheper-Hughes, N. 1992. *Death without weeping: The violence of everyday life in Brazil*. University of California Press.

Schilt, K. 2010. *Just one of the guys? Transgender men and the persistence of gender inequality*. University of Chicago Press.

Schilt, K., & Westbrook, L. 2009. Doing gender, doing heteronormativity: "Gender normals," transgender people, and the social maintenance of heterosexuality. *Gender and Society*, *23*(4), 440–464.

Scott, W. R. 2013. *Institutions and organizations: Ideas, interests, and identities*. Sage.

Sedgwick, E. K. 2008. *Epistemology of the closet*. University of California Press.

Seidman, S. 2004. *Beyond the closet: The transformation of gay and lesbian life*. Psychology Press.

Serovich, J. M., Grafsky, E. L., & Craft, S. M. 2011. Does family matter to HIV-positive men who have sex with men? *Journal of Marital and Family Therapy*, *37*(3), 290–298.

Shedd, C. 2015. *Unequal city: Race, schools, and perceptions of injustice*. Russell Sage Foundation.

shuster, s. m. 2017. Punctuating accountability: How discursive aggression regulates transgender people. *Gender and Society*, *31*(4), 481–502.

Silva, J. M. 2013. *Coming up short: Working-class adulthood in an age of uncertainty.* Oxford University Press.

Simmons-Duffin, S. 2020. Transgender health protections reversed by Trump administration. National Public Radio. https://www.npr.org

Skinner, D. A., & Kohler, J. K. 2002. Parental rights in diverse family contexts: Current legal developments. *Family Relations, 51*(4), 293–300.

Solebello, N., & Elliott, S. 2011. "We want them to be as heterosexual as possible": Fathers talk about their teen children's sexuality. *Gender and Society, 25*(3), 293–315.

Stacey, J. 1998. *Brave new families: Stories of domestic upheaval in late-twentieth-century America.* University of California Press.

Stacey, L. 2021. The family as gender and sexuality factory: A review of the literature and future directions. *Sociology Compass,* e12864.

Stacey, L., & Padavic, I. 2020. Complicating parents' gender and sexual expectations for children: A comparison of biological parents and stepparents. *Sexualities,* 1363460720906988.

Stack, C. B., & Burton, L. M. 1993. Kinscripts. *Journal of Comparative Family Studies, 24*(2), 157–170.

Stone, A. L. 2018. The geography of research on LGBTQ life: Why sociologists should study the South, rural queers, and ordinary cities. *Sociology Compass, 12*(11), e12638.

Stone, A. L. 2020. When my parents came to the gay ball: Comfort work in adult child–parent relationships. *Journal of Family Issues,* 0192513X20935497.

Stone, A. L., Nimmons, E., & Davis, S. R. 2019. *"I will cut them out": Family estrangement as a resilience strategy for transgender and non-binary adults.* [Paper presentation]. American Sociological Association annual meeting, New York, New York, United States.

Stone, L. 1979. *The family: Sex and marriage in England 1500–1800.* Penguin.

Stryker, S. 2008. Transgender history, homonormativity, and disciplinarity. *Radical History Review, 2008*(100), 145–157.

Sumerau, J. E., & Mathers, L. A. 2019. *America through transgender eyes.* Rowman and Littlefield.

Sumerau, J. E., Mathers, L. A., & Moon, D. 2020. Foreclosing fluidity at the intersection of gender and sexual normativities. *Symbolic Interaction, 43*(2), 205–234.

Sutfin, E. L., Fulcher, M., Bowles, R. P., & Patterson, C. J. 2008. How lesbian and heterosexual parents convey attitudes about gender to their children: The role of gendered environments. *Sex Roles, 58*(7–8), 501–513.

Tan, C. K. 2011. Go home, gay boy! Or, why do Singaporean gay men prefer to "go home" and not "come out"? *Journal of Homosexuality, 58*(6–7), 865–882.

Taylor, R. J., Chatters, L. M., Woodward, A. T., & Brown, E. 2013. Racial and ethnic differences in extended family, friendship, fictive kin, and congregational informal support networks. *Family Relations, 62*(4), 609–624.

Thompson, L., & Walker, A. J. 1995. The place of feminism in family studies. *Journal of Marriage and Family, 57*(4), 847–865.

Titlestad, A., & Pooley, J. A. 2014. Resilience in same-sex-parented families: The lived experience of adults with gay, lesbian, or bisexual parents. *Journal of GLBT Family Studies, 10*(4), 329–353.

Tobia, J. 2016. Everything you ever wanted to know about gender neutral pronouns. *Time.* https://time.com

Todres, J., & Villamizar Fink, D. 2020. The trauma of Trump's family separation and child detention actions: A children's rights perspective. *Washington Law Review,* 95(1), 3777–3827.

Travers, A. 2019. *The trans generation: How trans kids (and their parents) are creating a gender revolution.* NYU Press.

Troiden, R. R. 1989. The formation of homosexual identities. *Journal of Homosexuality,* 17(1–2), 43–74.

Troiden, R. R., & Goode, E. 1980. Variables related to the acquisition of a gay identity. *Journal of Homosexuality,* 5(4), 383–392.

Tuthill, Z. 2016. Negotiating religiosity and sexual identity among Hispanic lesbian mothers. *Journal of Homosexuality* 63(9), 1194–1210.

Vangelisti, A. L. 2006. Relationship dissolution: Antecedents, processes, and consequences. In P. Noller & J. A. Feeney (Eds.), *Close relationships: Functions, forms, and processes* (pp. 353–374). Psychology Press.

Vega, W. A. 1995. *The study of Latino families: A point of departure.* Sage.

Ward, D. E. 2009. *The white welfare state: The racialization of US welfare policy.* University of Michigan Press.

Ward, J. 2020. *The tragedy of heterosexuality.* NYU Press.

Warner, M. 2000. *The trouble with normal: Sex, politics, and the ethics of queer life.* Harvard University Press.

Watson, J. B. 2014. Bisexuality and family: Narratives of silence, solace, and strength. *Journal of GLBT Family Studies 10*(1–2), 101–123.

Watson, R. J., Rose, H. A., Doull, M., Adjei, J., & Saewyc, E. 2019. Worsening perceptions of family connectedness and parent support for lesbian, gay, and bisexual adolescents. *Journal of Child and Family Studies,* 28(11), 3121–3131.

Weeks, J., Heaphy, B., & Donovan, C. 2001. *Same sex intimacies: Families of choice and other life experiments.* Psychology Press.

West, A., Lewis, J., Roberts, J., & Noden, P. 2017. Young adult graduates living in the parental home: Expectations, negotiations, and parental financial support. *Journal of Family Issues,* 38(17), 2449–2473.

West, C., & Zimmerman, D. H. 1987. Doing gender. *Gender and Society, 1*(2), 125–151.

Weston, K. 1997. *Families we choose: Lesbians, gays, kinship.* Columbia University Press.

White, C. 2006. Federally mandated destruction of the Black family: The Adoption and Safe Families Act. *Northwestern Journal of Law and Social Policy,* (1)1, 303–337.

Witt, S. D. 1997. Parental influence on children's socialization to gender roles. *Adolescence,* 32(126), 253–259.

Wood, E., Desmarais, S., & Gugula, S. 2002. The impact of parenting experience on gender stereotyped toy play of children. *Sex Roles*, *47*(1–2), 39–49.

Yip, Andrew K. T. 1997. Dare to differ: Gay and lesbian Catholics' assessment of official Catholic positions on sexuality. *Sociology of Religion* 58(2), 165–180.

Yu, V. 2010. Shelter and transitional housing for transgender youth. *Journal of Gay and Lesbian Mental Health*, *14*(4), 340–345.

Zaloom, C. 2019. *Indebted: How families make college work at any cost*. Princeton University Press.

Zelizer, V. 1985. *Pricing the priceless child: The changing social value of children*. Duyan, Ankara.

Zimman, L. 2009. "The other kind of coming out": Transgender people and the coming out narrative genre. *Gender and Language*, *3*(1), 53–80.

Zinn, M. B. 1982. Familism among Chicanos: A theoretical review. *Humboldt Journal of Social Relations*, *10*(1), 224–238.

Zinn, M. B. 1998. Family, feminism, and race in America. In K. V. Hansen & A. I. Garey (Eds.), *Families in the US: Kinship and domestic politics* (pp. 33–41). Temple University Press.

INDEX

Italic page numbers refer to tables

ABOUT THE AUTHORS

RIN RECZEK is Professor of Sociology at The Ohio State University. Rin is the author of more than sixty articles and book chapters, most of which are on LGBTQ families, and is the co-editor of *Marriage and Health: The Well-Being of Same-Sex Couples*.

EMMA BOSLEY-SMITH is a doctoral candidate in sociology at The Ohio State University. Her work focuses on class, gender, and sexuality, with a special focus on economic insecurity among LGBTQ young adults.